Thomas E.
and Sisters

compiled by

Lawrence S. Saxon

SPONSOR

MRS. THOMAS E. FRASER

Library of Congress Catalog
Card Number: Applied for.
ISBN: 978-1-56311-334-5

Additional copies may be purchased directly
from the publisher.

CHRISTENING DM - 24

10 June 1944

*This book is dedicated to the
officers and men who earned a place of honor in history
and gave their lives for their country while serving in the
Naval Minewarfare Service during World War II.*

Lawrence S. Saxon enlisted in the US Navy on 5 July 1946. Completing training at the US Naval Training Center at Bainbridge, Maryland with Company # 4636 at the 318L barracks, he was assigned to the USS Thomas E. Fraser DM-24, a destroyer minelayer of the Sumner Class. His duties were with the Engineering Department serving in the forward fireroom. With 21 months sea duty and completion of his Naval service, 2 July 1948, he went into the civilian world working for the Westinghouse Electric Corporation at the firms Pittsburgh R & D Center as an Equipment Coordinator in the Semi-Conductor field. He obtain a Commercial Instrument Pilots rating and saw much of his Navy port of calls from the air in the islands. Upon retiring from industry, photography became a hobby which lead to many of the photographs obtained for this book.

courtsey of BIW

Commander THOMAS EDWARD FRASER

He is a concoction of all ages, all races and all men.

In him are combined, none too harmoniously, it is true, the fatalism of the Orient, the " joie de vivre " of the French, the American's weakness for " Best Sellers " and the blarney of Erin.

He delights in disorder, and is contemptuous of method.

He early learned the futility of making love on strictly truthful principles, yet frankly admits that he is not susceptible to flattery.

He is somewhat of a literateur, but modesty alone prevents the publication of " My Ascent of Mount Pelee ", or " The Value of Stimulants to the Explorer ", and " Perfect Behavior for the Bacchant ".

Second Class Christmas leave caused him to take more than a professional interest in art, in fact, he maintains that the expression "Art for art's sake" should be changed to "Art for the artist's sake".

Suggest a game of bridge and he proudly points to the crossed spades on the family crest. His expression, " Labor ipse voluptas ", will always be reminiscent of his industry.

courtsey of the "Lucky Bag", United States Naval Academy

November 14th., 1942

Savo Island, Guadalcanal

Task Force 64

Rear Adm. Willis A. Lee

Battleships:

Washington	BB-56	Capt. Glenn B. Davis
South Dakota	BB-57	Capt. Thomas L. Gatch

Destroyers

Walke	DD-416	Cdr. Thomas E. Fraser
Benham	DD-397	Lt. Cdr. John B. Taylor
Preston	DD-379	Cdr. Max C. Stormes
Gwin	DD-433	Lt. Cdr. John B. Fellows Jr.

National Archives

USS WALKE (DD-416)

USS *Walke* (DD-416) was laid down on 31 May 1938 at the Boston Navy Yard ; launched on 20 October 1939 ; sponsored by Mrs. Clarence Dillon, grandniece of the late Rear Admiral Walke ; and commissioned on 27 April 1940, Lt. Comdr. Carl H. Sanders in command.

Walke's active service had begun in the spring of 1940 when Germany was unleashing her military might in Norway and the lowlands of western Europe to turn the so-called " Phony War " into the blitzkrieg which swept across northern France, driving British troops off the continent and knocking France out of the war. The resulting establishment of a new government in that country, more favorable to Germany, aroused fear in Allied and neutral circles that French fighting forces, particularly French warships, might be placed in German hands. *Walke* would have a role in seeing that this unfortunate development would never take place.

After fueling at San Juan on the 6th, the destroyer got underway on the afternoon of the following day on " Caribbean Patrol " in company with sistership *O'Brien* (DD-415). Rendezvousing with *Moffett* (DD-362) and *Sims* (DD-409) off Fort de France, Martinique, *Walke* and *O'Brien* patrolled the approaches to that port, keeping an eye on the movements of the Vichy French warships-the auxiliary cruisers *Barfleur* and *Quercy* and the aircraft carrier *Beam* - through 14 December. *Walke* then visited Port Castries, British West Indies, on the 15th and embarked Comdr. Lyman K. Swenson, Commander, Destroyer Division 17, who hoisted his pennant in her that day.

Walke then patrolled off the Atlantic coast between Norfolk and Newport well into June, as the Atlantic Fleet's neutrality patrols were steadily extended eastward, closer to the European war zone. She departed Newport on 27 July and screened a convoy to Iceland, reaching Reykjavik on 6 August and turning toward Norfolk the same day, her charges safely delivered.

The destroyer subsequently returned to those northern climes in mid-September- after local operations in the Newport-Boston area-reaching Hvalfjordur on 14 September. She operated in Icelandic waters into late September, before she put into Argentia, Newfoundland, on 11 October, en route to Casco Bay, Maine. She began an overhaul at the Boston Navy Yard on 25 November and completed it on 7 December, the " day of infamy " on which Japan attacked Pearl Harbor and thrust the United States into war in the Pacific. Departing the yard on that day, *Walke* reached Norfolk on 12 December, via Casco Bay, and remained there until the 16th when she sailed for the Panama Canal and the Pacific.

After reaching San Diego , Calif., on 30 December, *Walke* sailed with the newly formed Task Force (TF) 17 bound for the South Pacific, on 6 January 1942, screening *Yorktown* (CV-5) as that carrier covered the movement of reinforcements for the Marine garrision on American Samoa. The convoy subsequently arrived at Tutuila on 24 January. However, TF 17 remained in Samoan waters for only a short time, for it soon sailed north for the Marshalls-Gilberts area to deliver the first offensive blow to the enemy, only eight weeks after the bombing of Pearl Harbor.

Walke served in the antisubmarine screen and plane guarded for the *Yorktown* as that carrier launched air strikes on suspected Japanese installations on the atolls of Jaluit, Makin, and Milli. Although Admiral Chester W. Nimitz, the Commander in Chief, Pacific Fleet (CinCPAC), considered the raids " well-conceived, well planned, and brilliantly executed," the damage they actually caused was not as great as reported ; and, outside of the boost they gave to American morale, the attacks were only a minor nuisance to the Japanese. Nevertheless, the American Fleet had finally taken the war to the enemy.

Returning to Hawaiian waters on 7 February, *Walke* trained in the Hawaiian area until 27 February, when she sailed for the Ellice Islands. She later exercised with TF 17 off New Caledonia in early March before she sailed, again screening *Yorktown*, for the New Guinea area , as part of the force put together to check Japanese expansion in that area.

By that time, the enemy advance to the southward, in the New Guinea-New Britain area, had gained considerable momentum with the occupation of Rabaul and Gasmata, New Britain; Kavieng, New Ireland ; and on sites on Bougainville in the Solomons and in the Louisiades. By the end of February 1942, it seemed probable that the Japanese were planning to mount an offensive in early March. TF 11 and TF 17 were dispatched to the area. Vice Admiral Wilson Brown, in overall charge of the operation, initially selected Rabaul and Gasmata, in New Britain and Kavieng, in New Ireland , as targets for the operation.

Walke then screened *Yorktown* as she launched air strikes on Tulagi in the Solomons on 4 May and later separated from the carrier with the " Support Force " - the Australian heavy cruiser HMAS *Australia*, a light cruiser HMAS *Hobart*, and the American destroyers *Farragut* (DD-348) and *Perkins* (DD-377) - to protect the southern mouth of the Jomard Passage. On the afternoon of 7 May, Japanese Aichi D3A1 " Val " divebombers attacked the formation, but the heavy antiaircraft fire thrown up by the ships caused the enemy to retire without scoring any hits.

An hour after the " Vals " departed, however, Japanese twin-engined bombers appeared and made a torpedo attack from dead ahead. Again, a heavy volume of antiaircraft fire from *Walke* and the other destroyers peppered the skies. Five bombers splashed into the sea, and no torpedoes found their mark on the Allied ships. Later, 19 high altitude bombers passed over, dropping sticks of bombs that splashed harmlessly into the water. Antiaircraft fire proved ineffective, due to the high altitude maintained by the planes. However, the last group of planes were apparently American planes. The force commander, Rear Admiral John G. Crace, Royal Navy, swore that the planes were B-26's ; *Walke's* commander, Comdr. Thomas E. Fraser, subsequently reported them to be B-17's. In any event, it was fortunate that the bombardiers were not too accurate.

On 7 March, Allied intelligence learned that a Japanese surface force- including transports-lay off Buna, New Guinea. On the following day, Japanese troops went ashore at Lae and Salamaua, New Guinea, and secured those places by noon.

Three days later, *Yorktown* and *Lexington* launched air strikes against the newly established

Japanese beachheads at Lae and Salamaua. The attack took the enemy by surprise. The planes from the two American flattops came in from over the Owen Stanley Mountains and inflicted damage on ships, small craft, and shore installations, before they retired.

Walke remained at sea with the *Yorktown* task force into April. Detached to escort *Ramsay* (DM-16) and *Sumner* (AG-32), the destroyer reached Suva, in the Fiji Islands, on 19 April and got underway the next day bound for the Tonga Islands. Reaching Tongatabu on the 22d, *Walke* fueled from *Kaskaskia* (AO-27) before she underwent boiler repairs and loaded depth charges prior to her return to TF 17.

Detached from the group because of a damaged starboard reduction gear, *Walke* headed to Australia for repairs and reached Brisbane on 12 May. Upon completion of the work on 29 May, the destroyer ran trials in the Brisbane River before being pronounced fit for service and sailed for New Caledonia on 9 June.

Arriving at Noumea on 13 June, *Walke* fueled there before proceeding via Tongatabu to Pago Pago, Samoa. Assigned to Task Group (TG) 12.1, the destroyer sailed on 26 June for Bora Bora in the Society Islands. With the dissolution of TG 12.1 on 11 July, *Walke* then reported for duty to Commander TG 6.7-the commanding officer of *Castor* (AKS-1) . She then escorted *Castor* to San Francisco, Calif., arriving there on 2 August.

On 7 August, while *Walke* was undergoing repairs and alterations at the Mare Island Navy Yard, the United States Navy wrested the initiative in the war from Japan by landing marines on Guadalcanal in the Solomon Islands. In ensuing months, the armed forces of the two nations struggled mightily for control of that island chain. The contest soon developed into a logistics race as each side tried to frustrate its opponent's efforts to reinforce and supply his forces fighting on Guadalcanal while doing all in his power to strengthen his own. *Walke's* future was to be inextricably tied to the almost daily-and nightly-American air and naval attempts to best the Japanese in their thrust down " The Slot ", the strategic body of water which stretches between the two lines of islands which make up the Solomon chain and lead to Guadalcanal.

Completing the yard work on 25 August, *Walke* ran her trials in San Francisco Bay and that day received orders to proceed to San Pedro, Calif., to rendezvous with the oiler *Kankakee* (AO-39) and escort her from the west coast of the United States- Via Noumea, New Caledonia- to Tongatabu, arriving there on 9 September. The destroyer later escorted a convoy consisting of *Kankakee*, *Navajo* (AT-64), and *Arctic* (AF-7) from Tomgatabu to Noumea, where she prepared for action in the Solomons.

About sunset on 13 November, the day after the Naval Battle of Guadalcanal began, *Walke* sortied with TF 64 which was built around the fast battleships *Washington* (BB-56) and *South Dakota* (BB-57) and -besides *Walke* - was screened by *Preston* (DD-337), *Gwin* (DD433), and *Benham* (DD-397). By late in the forenoon on the 14th, TF 64 had reached a point some 50 miles south-by-west from Guadalcanal.

Sighted by the enemy- who reported them as one battleship, one cruiser, and four destroyers-the American warships spent most of the day on the 14th avoiding contact with enemy planes. From the information available in dispatches, the commander of the American task force, Rear Admiral Willis Augustus Lee, knew of the presence of three groups of enemy ships in the area, one of which was formed around at least two battleships.

Proceeding through the flat calm sea and disposed in column with *Walke* leading, the American ships approached on a northerly course about nine miles west of Guadalcanal.

Lee's ships continued making their passage, picking up Japanese voice transmissions on the radio while the ships radar " eyes " scanned the darkness. At 0006 on 15 November, *Washington* received a report that indicated the presence of three ships, rounding the north end of Savo Island, heading westward.   Almost simultaneously the flagship's radar picked up two ships on the same bearing.

Ten minutes later, *Washington* opened fire with her 16-inch guns; and within seconds, *South Dakota* followed suit. *Walke* opened fire at 0026, maintaining a rapid barrage at what probably was the Japanese light cruiser *Nagara*. After checking fire within a few minutes, the lead destroyer opened up again at a Japanese destroyer 7,500 yards to starboard and , later, at gunflashes off her port side near Guadalcanal.

Japanese shells straddled *Walke* twice, and then a " Long Lance " torpedo slammed into her starboard side at a point directly below mount 52. Almost simultaneously, a salvo of shells from one of the Japanese light cruisers hurtled down upon the hapless destroyer, a deluge of steel that struck home with devastating effect in the radio room, the foremast, below the gig davits, and in the vicinity of mount 53, on the after deckhouse. Meanwhile the torpedo had blown off the bow of the ship ; and fire broke out as the forward 20-millimeter magazine blew up.

With the situation hopeless, Comdr. Thomas E. Fraser, *Walke's* commanding officer, ordered the ship abandoned. As the destroyer sank rapidly by the bow, only two life rafts could be launched. The others had been damaged irreparably. After the crew made sure that the depth charges were set on safe, they went over the side just before the ship slipped swiftly under the surface.

As *Washington* - dueling with the Japanese battleship *Kirishima* and smaller ships-swept through the flotsam and jetsam of battle, she briefly noted *Walke's* plight and that of *Preston*, which had also gone down under in a deluge of shells. At 0041-just a minute or so before *Walke's* battered form sank beneath the waves of the waters off Savo Island into " Ironbottom Sound " - life rafts from the battleship splashed into the sea for the benefit of the survivors. Although the destroyer's depth charges had apparently been set to " safe " , some depth charges went off killing a number of swimming survivors and seriously injuring others. As the battle went on ahead of them, the able-bodied survivors placed their more seriously wounded comrades on rafts.

Walke's survivors were , at one point, in two groups- some clinging to the still-floating bow section and others clustered around the two rafts that the ship had been able to launch. During the harrowing night, they were twice illuminated by enemy warships but not molested, before the enemy switched off his searchlights and moved on.

At dawn, however, *Walke's* survivors - and those from *Preston* - witnessed the end of a quartet of Japanese transports beached during the night. Bombed and strafed by Army, Marine, and Navy planes - including aircraft from " The Big E "- *Enterprise* (CV-6) - the four Japanese ships received the *coup de grace* from *Meade* (DD-571) that morning, just before the destroyer altered course and picked up the destroyermen from *Walke* and *Preston*.

Meade rescued 151 men from *Walke*, six of whom later died after they were brought ashore at Tulagi. Six officers - including Comdr. Fraser - and 76 men had died in the ships fiery end off Savo Island. Cmdr. Fraser was posthumously awarded the Navy Cross for his valor and devotion to duty. *Walke* was struck from the Navy list on 13 January 1943.

Walke received three battle stars for her World War II service.

IRONBOTTOM SOUND SHIPS

USS WALKE (DD416)   <u>CRH REVISION</u>, 7 June 1992

SUNK by Torpedo & Gunfire,   Naval Battle of Guadalcanal, 14 November 1942

" SIMS " Class Destroyer. Launched 20 October 1939.

Length: 347'11" ; Beam: 36'1" Hull Depth: 21' to main deck: 28.5' to forecastle. Disp: 1620 tons.

WRECK LOCATION: (Morison-chart) -- 09 12.3 ' S,   159 45.5 ' E
(FRANK-chart) -- about 09 13+ ' S, 159 43+ 'E
(GWIN Action Report) -- See below...essentially as Morison.

DAMAGE DISCRIPTION:

(MORISON) -- At about 2330, *Walke* was struck by enemy shells and began to fall off to port,
shooting furiously and endeavoring to get onto the target with her torpedos. ... at 2338
enemy warheads began to find their marks. *Walke* had her forecastle blown off as far aft
as the bridge". "*Walke*, dismembered and blazing, was down by the head and sinking
fast. ... the after two-thirds of the ship sank at 2342 and depth charges ... exploded directly
under the survivors." 135 survivors rescued next day.
(DANFS) -- Opened fire at 0026, "maintaining a rapid barrage on what probably was ...
Nagara". Checked fire briefly, then opened on a Japanese DD 7500 yards to starboard
and " at gunflashes off her port side near Guadalcanal". "Japanese shells straddled *Walke*
twice" then a torpedo hit her starboard "almost directly below mount 52", blowing off her
bow. Forward 20mm magazine blew up and started a fire. Salvo of shells from Japanese
CL hit radio room, foremast, "below the gig davits", and on/in after deck house near mount
53. Abandon ship ordered as *Walke* sank rapidly by the bow, with only two rafts
launched (others damaged "irreparably") .
Some depth charges went off , killing and injuring survivors. Bow section remained afloat
and survivors clung to it.
(FRANK) -- Only U.S. DD with operational FD fire control radar. Opened fire at 2322 on
Ayanami. Shifted fire about 2327 to *Nagara* and her consorts. "*Walke* was reeling
from gunfire hits when a Long Lance impacted just foreward of her bridge. The sympathetic
detonation of *Walke's* number two magazine vastly magnified the formidable power of the
torpedo's large warhead. The blast seemed to lift the whole ship and shove her to port. The
bow snapped off, power and communications failed, the main deck was awash with several
inches of oil from ruptured fuel tanks, and flames scampered along what was left of
Walke's length. With ammunition exploding and the ship settling rapidly ... " CO ordered
abandonment. Depth charges exploded as she sank, killing men in the water.
Washington dropped rafts to floating survivors as she passed. Survivors watched
Japanese transports arrive and run aground around 0400.
(DULL) -- "*Walke*, hit repeatedly by gunfire, began to lose way to port; then, at 2338, a torpedo
ripped into her , and she sank four minutes later".
(HAMMEL) -- After increasing speed to 26 kts., spotted *Ayanami* and *Uranami* "dead ahead" off
south end of Savo. FD radar blinded by land return. Opened fire with forward 5" mounts at
range of 11,000 yards. After "several minutes" , she saw a "fresh target" against Savo, off
her forward bow, range 7500 yards and shifted fire to it. Reported hits but lost target around
a point of land.

Straddled twice by shells at about 2330, while turning to port to launch her own torpedos. "Seconds later" torpedo wake seen approaching. torpedo hit directly under 5" mount # 2. Quickly thereafter, hit by gunfire in radio shack, foremast and "all around" 5" mount # 3. Torpedo tore off bow back to bridge, detonated 20mm magazine and opened forward fireroom to sea. Fires seen around and forward of bridge. Speed of ship drove her under. *Benham* reported *Walke* was "well down by the head" and being abandoned by some men as she passed. CO ordered ship abandoned. Officers on bridge reported mount # 4 still firing as he prepared to abandon.

At 2342 *Walke* "stood straight up out of the water, hung for a few seconds, and then disappeared from view, stern last". Bow section twisted loose and came to surface, allowing men from mount # 1 and its handling room to escape. Bow remained afloat and men used it as a float. At 2343, depth charges exploded under the survivors. *Washington* dropped life rafts as she passed through the survivors.

Tide carried survivors towards Guadalcanal shore. Japanese submarine surfaced among them about an hour after *Walke* sank, illuminated survivors but did nothing further. About an hour before dawn, two Japanese transports passed nearby and anchored "several hundred yards out from the nearby beach". After daylight, some survivors were fired on by riflemen on the beach, and swam out of range. Transports reported beached at Doma Cove by plane, which also saw *Walke's* bow and groups of survivors. USS *Meade* and boats from Lunga Point rescued swimmers in mid-late afternoon. Three men from *Walke* killed after rescue by a Japanese air attack.

(BuSHIPS Damage Summary) -- "Struck by cruiser salvo. Destroyer torpedo struck frame 45 starboard. Bow blown off forward of bridge. Stern section plunged. Depth charges exploded. Bow remained afloat and finally sank". (see drawing for location of hits).

(WALKE Action Report) -- Ship had been straddled twice before torpedo hit and was struck by "apparent cruiser gunfire" after torpedo explosion. Shells hit radio room, foremast, under gig davits and in vicinity of gun # 3. Bulkhead of forward fireroom buckled as was main deck amidships.

(GWIN Action Report) -- Shows northerly track chart, with ships essentially on same tracks as Morison's chart.

(MEADE Action Report) -- Shows survivors floating in area due south of Savo Island, roughly between 1 to 4.25 miles south of island and 3 miles wide. This encompasses the sinking position for *Preston* shown on Morison chart and is about 2 miles east of position shown there for *Walke* sinking.

CASUALTIES: 6 officers and 76 men lost with ship.
(FRANK) ---------80 killed, 48 injured.
(WALKE Action Report) -- 6 officers and 76 men killed or missing.

IDENTIFICATION POINTS:
Walke's sunken after portion should be readily identifiable by standard features of her class, especially her single set of uptakes with two quad torpedo tube mounts behind. She is probably severely damaged at the stern and/or by the after deckhouse by depth charge explosions.

Her bow should lie quite a distance away, possibly near the Guadalcanal shore. It may have # 1 5" gun mount attached.

FUTURE EXAMINATION:
Walke is only a "last priority" target for our expedition's search, and it is doubtful if we will get to her. It is even more doubtful that we will search for her bow. If we do find her, she should receive sufficient imaging for identification and evaluation of her condition.

If found, she would make a valuable contribution to understanding the November 14-15 action, and also would make a dramatically useful companion to *KIRISHIMA.*

USS WALKE (DD-416) -- ANTICIPATED CONFIGURATION OF WRECK

C.R. Haberlein Jr., Naval Historical Center, 10/96

Based on damage reportedly received by the ship during the Naval Battle of Guadalcanal, plus general details of other shipwrecks examined during the 1991-92 Iron Bottom Sound Expedition.

" Summary of War Damage "

BOW SECTION PROBABLY LOCATED QUITE SOME DISTANCE FROM REST OF SHIP WRECKAGE. IT PROBABLY EXTENDS AFT TO INCLUDE # 1 5" GUN.

TORPEDO HIT, AND POSSIBLE DETONATION OF SOME AMMUNITION IN # 2 5" GUN'S MAGAZINE, SEVERS BOW AS FAR BACK AS THE BRIDGE, DESTROYING HULL AND SUPERSTRUCTURE IN THE VICINITY OF # 2 5" GUN.

WALKE'S after portion will probably be upright on the sea floor. Her bow section will be lying on one side or the other.

GUNS, GUN DIRECTOR AND TORPEDO TUBES WILL BE TRAINED TO STARBOARD.

STACK & FOREMAST WILL BE COLLAPSED (AND/OR MISSING ALTOGETHER) DUE TO POST-SINKING WATER PRESSURE.

⊗.... POSSIBLE LOCATION OF JAPANESE SHELL HITS.

Possible "Mud" line

DAMAGE TO STERN, AND POSSIBLY AFTER DECKHOUSE, FROM DEPTH CHARGE EXPLOSIONS AFTER SHIP SANK.

Since WALKE'S wreck is probably located in the strong tidal scouring area between Savo Island and Guadalcanal, it is possible that she is not deeply sunken in bottom sediment. There may be implosion damage aft, caused by her rapid sinking. There will be extensive corrosion of her light sheet metal structure, some marine growth, and sediment deposits on horizontal surfaces.

9

VESSELS LOST

DESTROYERS (continued)

Ship	Date	Place	Cause	Manner of Sinking	Remarks on Damage
BENHAM (DD397)	11/15/42	Guadalcanal	DD Torp.-1	Sunk by gunfire from GWIN	Struck on starboard bow about frame 6 by destroyer torpedo. Bow destroyed forward of frame 14. Flexural vibration resulted in buckling of shell plating and longitudinals at frame 75. Began to break up. Sunk by own forces. 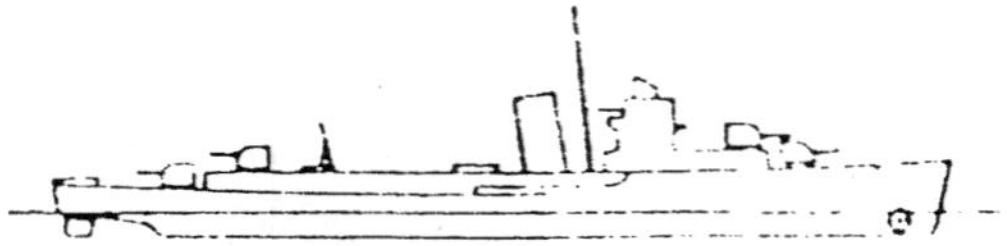
PRESTON (DD379)	11/15/42	Guadalcanal	Gunfire - 5	Listed to stbd. until on beam's end, then plunged by stern.	Struck on starboard side by two 6" projectiles between No. 1 and No. 2 firerooms. Fires were started which set torpedo warheads on fire. Hit on port side amidships by about 3 projectiles. 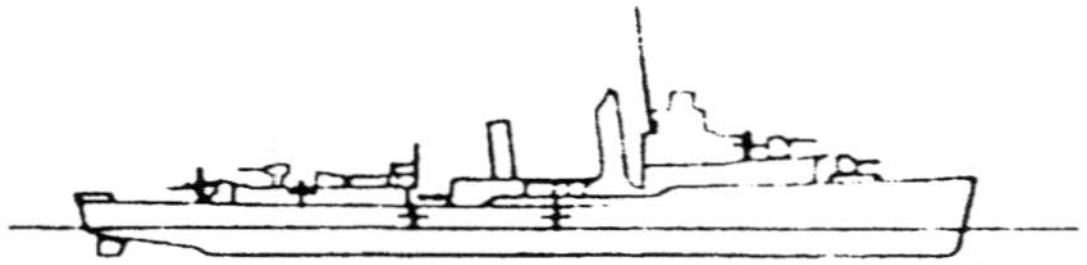
WALKE (DD416)	11/15/42	Guadalcanal	Gunfire DD Torp.-1	Bow broke off and floated, remainder sank bow first.	Struck by cruiser salvo. Destroyer torpedo struck frame 45 starboard. Bow blown off forward of bridge. Stern section plunged. Depth charges exploded. Bow remained afloat and finally sank. 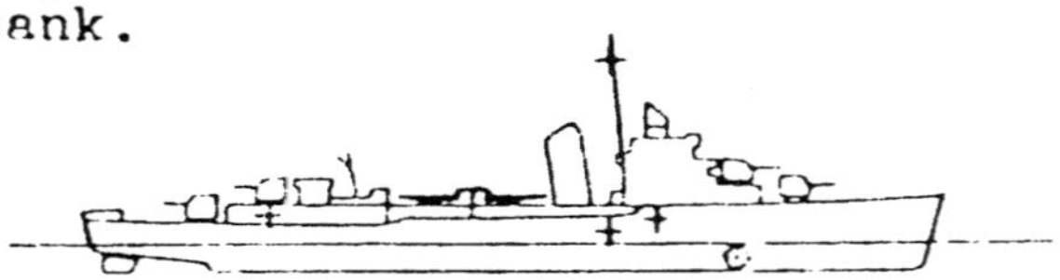

10

USS Thomas E. Fraser (DM-24)
1400, 22 August 1944
Charleston Navy Yard, Boston, MA.

ORDER OF EVENTS

The Commanding Officer, Commander C.A. Johnson, U.S. Navy, meets Rear Admiral R.A. Theobald, U.S. Navy, Commandant of the Boston Navy Yard and of the First Naval District, and Captain R.C. Grady, U.S. Navy (Ret.), Captain of the Yard.

The Commanding officer reports to the Captain of the Yard that all is in readiness for the Commissioning Ceremony.

The Captain of the Yard requests permission from the Commandant to proceed with the Commissioning.

The Captain of the Yard directs that the ship be placed in Commission.

All hands face in the direction the colors are to be hoisted.

The band plays the " National Anthem ". Colors are hoisted and the Admiral's Flag broken.

The Commanding Officer reads his orders and assumes Command.

The Admiral's Flag is broken.

The first watch is set.

Address by the Commandant.

The Commanding Officer delivers a message from the Secretary of the Navy.

The Chaplain delivers the invocation.

The Commandant makes a brief inspection and departs.

The Commission Pennant replaces the Admiral's Flag.

The ceremony is completed

" if the ship is half as good a ship as Tommy was a man -
it will be the fightingest ship in this or any man's navy. "

Captain HARTWIG, USN (a classmate of Comdr. THOMAS E. FRASER)
10 June 1944   Bath Iron Works, Bath, Maine.

courtest of BIW

Launching of USS Thomas E. Fraser (DD-736) 10 June 1944
Down the ways, slip 2, Bath Iron Works, Bath, Maine.

THE SAGA OF THE THOMAS E. FRASER (DM 24)
by John C. Roach SOM 1c

EVOLUTION :

We are a new ship and we bare the name of a fighting man. We are also a new crew but many of us are veterans of major engagements when we served with other units of the fleet. Yes we are a new ship and a new crew, but with the spirit that is as old as any tradition of the Navy.

A light minelayer, she, the ship, is known as. Placed in the category of a non combatant ship as are all minecraft. Placed in this category only because all minelayers are so placed. But we, the crew know different, for we can see by her size and armament that she is more than a match for any similar type of craft in any navy of this world. We also know that the Navy has recognized this fact and also that we are more than a match for a number of our own ships that are playing major rolls in this terrible war.

Though we were born in the non combatant class and that in name we shall stay within the class as long as we remain a minelayer. We also know that the Navy will make use of our power by using us for operations that require the use of a ship of a combat class. Of course we realize that we shall be used as such, only when our duties as a minelayer are temporarily not needed.

There are twelve ships, all new ships, all of the same formidable type built in various ship yards stretching from the East to the West coasts. The twelve of us shall form a squadron and within the squadron shall be three divisions, each division containing four ships. Our division contains the *Bauer*, *Fraser*, *Shannon* and *Smith*.

COMMISSIONING AND PREPARATION :

We were placed in commission on a bright, warm day on the twenty-second of August in the year nineteen forty four. The site of the ceremony was the CHARLESTON NAVY YARD in BOSTON, MASSACHUSETTS. The assemblage was small consisting only of close relatives of the crew and interested laymen. The ceremony was impressive and brief in keeping with the customs of wartime conditions.

We stayed in Boston for well over a month while we made the new ship ready for sea. Our time was limited and there was much to be done. The men had to be billeted and assigned to divisions and the assignment to battle stations, condition watches, abandon ship and fire and rescue stations are just a few of the problems that had to be solved for this ships crew of more than three hundred and fifty strong.

There were thousands of items to be brought aboard ranging in size from tremendous packing cases that were placed on board by large cranes to thumb tacks that were brought aboard inconspicuously. Items such as cooking utensils, heavy weather clothing, clerical supplies, gas masks, medical supplies, charts, electrical supplies are just a small minute, amount of the total that finally swelled the ship to the necessary level.

As the time sped quickly by, and the dock trials of the engines were already being conducted, it was a sure sign of the end of our fine life ashore. The calibration of our electrical equipment was suggested and accomplished before very long and our speed trials and the structural tests were not long in following. Then one bright morning we left all our friends ashore, and were off on our shakedown to prove our worth to the Navy.

THE SHAKEDOWN CRUISE :

It was the forth of October that we left dear old Boston and our destination was picturesque Bermuda. The few days of sailing were rough and the men to the sea kept diligently to their task of " feeding the fish. " Our shakedown was to be similar to an obstacle course and it was necessary to make every hurdle before the Fleets would accept you. It was a test both for the men and the ship and a very necessary one too, for it gave us the experience necessary to challenge the enemy when we came face to face, and we all knew that it would be beneficial.

Our stay at Bermuda was slightly over four weeks and it was a vigorous schedule that we held to. We would be at battle stations all day long and then find that we would be up half the night to carry out another operation necessary before final acceptance Fortunately the climate was ideal and though we were anchored within hailing distance of the beach, we were only permitted to go ashore once.

We endured the hardships and kept in mind the fact that we would soon be going back to Boston for a final checkup before leaving for combat. During our stay at Bermuda a few enemy submarines were reported or sighted within the area and twice we were ordered into port because one was reported in our vicinity. We were rather indignant that we could not seek out and destroy the sub if it were at all possible but orders are to be carried out, so we scurried back to the anchorage.

The final inspection was held and we were accepted by the Fleet, both the ship and crew passed every obstacle with flying colors and we left behind an enviable record that many a ship has attempted to attain. Our Captain, a Commander in the Navy Regulars, was thoroughly pleased with our performance and I assure you that he was the hardest of all to please.

Unfortunately we were ordered to Virginia for training in minelaying and we never did get back to Boston. It was truly discouraging for it was an ideal liberty port. We arrived at the Naval Mine Depot at Yorktown, Virginia and there we took on board a number of dummy mines. Our training operations were conducted in the Chesapeake Bay and lasted a little over a week.

At the conclusion of our training operations we were ordered to Portsmouth Navy Yard and there we underwent minor alterations and repairs. We were , at the time, assigned to the Pacific Fleet.

ASSIGNMENT :

We had our orders, every man in the crew knew it and yet not a one of us knew just what they were. Oh, it is true that we had all ascertained that we would be heading west. Yes we all knew that soon we would be going through the " Big Ditch " and into the blue Pacific but when, where or how? Those were the unanswered questions. Time apparently was going to be the only solution.

It was early morning that we slipped out of the Bay and the protective blanket of darkness was still securely wrapped around us. It was but a short time later that we were experiencing butterfly stomachs of a type that only Cape Hatteras is capable of dealing. Fortunately this ordeal was soon in passing and the water became a beautiful vivid expanse as we cruised along on a southerly course. Finally, the news was out that Guantanamo Bay, Cuba was our destination.

Cuba appeared above the horizon one early morning and though it was still early the weather was already sultry. After refueling and obtaining a small amount of supplies it was then close to noon and the weather was unbearable hot. From the unfair vantage point at which we had to observe Cuba, we found it discouraging and quite desolated and there was little anxiety for liberty from any of the crew. However a small portion of the crew did go ashore and they returned disappointed. Apparently our first impression of Cuba or Guantanamo was accurate.

A new, beautiful ship was at anchor in the harbor and we could see by her immensity and her formidable armament that she was a powerful lady. Her exceptionally sleek lines were very definite indications of high speed and her towering superstructure delivered a fairly strong resemblance to the pagoda type bridge of the Japanese battleships. However her bridge did not look as though it had been thrown together one piece on top of the other as in characteristic of the Japanese vessels.

It was learned shortly thereafter that this pride of the nation was the new super battle cruiser *Alaska* CB-1 , the newest major addition to the Navy's battle force and the first of her type. It was our assignment to escort her to San Diego, her destination. Therefore our stay in Cuba was quite brief and it was not very long after that we were approaching the Atlantic entrance to the PANAMA CANAL. We were proudly leading the way and showing to the world in general the impressive might that we were safe guarding.

It was at Panama that we were joined by the *Bauer* DM-26 and it was with her assistance that we escorted the *Alaska* CB-1 to San Diego.

THE CANAL ZONE :

To many of us the PANAMA CANAL ZONE was a new experience and the majority of us were out in the unbearable sun, just to make certain that we missed nothing of our strange surroundings. We stopped over night at the Atlantic entrance and liberty was announced for an estimated two thirds of the crew. We hastened into our immaculate liberty whites and left the filthy coal dock that we had the misfortune to tie up to, just as quickly as we could. A small water taxi was run for the convenience of the ships at the coal dock. It was nothing but a small dilapidated craft but it brought us across the narrow river. On the opposite bank were a number of taxies of a late American model and they whisked us into town, a fifteen minute ride, for fifty cents per person.

CRISTOBAL, yes here it is, surprisingly similar to motion pictures of the Panama Zone. It was quite apparent that the inhabitants of this city obtained their livelihood at the expense of tourists. The streets were brightly illuminated by the neon signs of the honky tonks. Every where to be found were bars, cafes and nightclubs. It became evident that these thriving cabbies drew concessions from the larger hotspots for dropping off their customers before their impressive entrances.

Intoxicants were not hard to be found in this wild town and imported liquors from just about every known country were to be found in quantity here for a nominal price.

It was a fast stepping, wild life that the crew enjoyed this night and most of us admitted that it was too fast for us. This town of fine liquors and brilliant signs had two aspects and the other aspect was not hard in finding. Here prostitution was legalized and you did not have to go seeking the large red light district that was just off the main section of this town. It was in this town that the women would come up to you and offer you their services for a fantastically cheap price. It was here the young girls from fourteen years of age to the old women over fifty would approach you and at times try by physical force to get you into their cheap, barely furnished rooms.

The red light district was immense and the methods of drawing customers were varied, forceful and amusing. The district was covered with filth as were their business establishments and it seemed odd to see the Christobal policemen who patrolled this area, watch the proceedings with approving eyes. Any man who has had at one time a spark of decency certainly knew better than to be coaxed into the filth that prevailed there.

PANAMA CANAL :

We started through the locks early the following morning and we had on board a congenial pilot who explained to us in detail the problems and other technical information and statistics that we all absorbed with a great amount of interest It took the complete day to go from the Atlantic to the Pacific side. At times we traveled through fresh water and the drop in buoyancy was noticeable on the *Bauer* for she was drawing quite a bit more water and traveling about five hundred yards astern of us. We took advantage of the fresh water by giving the ship a complete wash down. It proved beneficial for those men who had to stay below for it did cool the compartments, for they had been like a hot oven since early morning. The sun had been beating down on the metal plates with its intense rays.

It was a memorable trip and construction of new locks were located near at hand. It is hard to believe that man was capable of clearing out this tropical undergrowth and mountainous terrain and eventually construct the impressive sight that we observed that day. Finally the trip was over and we were out in the Pacific Ocean. We were informed at this point that we were now further west than when we entered the canal. I know that it is the fervent wish of all of us that not too long in the future we shall return and go through the canal from the Pacific to the Atlantic but of course the war must be won and the ruthless enemy destroyed.

The VOYAGE TO SAN DIEGO :

The weather was ideal and it was the smoothest expanse of water that I have ever had the opportunity to sail upon. It was quite warm this early day in December and many of us were glad we did not have to contend with the cold blast of the North Atlantic. We continued to conduct drills, and intensive training was carried on throughout the ship. It was necessary that every man reached the peak of his fighting efficiency.

The trip was uneventful and we had a number of opportunities to fire our batteries at aerial targets. It was apparent that the *Alaska* was very inexperienced although she was a superb fighting vessel. Even with her tremendous bulk she could at any moment put on a burst of speed and rapidly pull away from us and we could do nothing but look ridiculous. On one occasion we knocked down four out of five targets where as she knocked down one, out of twice the amount of opportunities that we had. At the time we were a great deal more accurate than she but it would not be long before she would excel us in her gunnery, for she had the necessary implements and in greater quantity. There is no doubt that she had the determination also.

We crept up the West Coast at a comfortable speed and finally sailed majestically into SAN DIEGO. What a teaming naval metropolis. Planes were lined up on the Naval Air Stations by the hundreds and ran well into the thousands. The city itself appeared to be very large and industrious and had a business-like atmosphere. We were assigned to a berth and we could hardly wait to get away on liberty.

OUR DAYS ON THE WEST COAST :

San Diego was found to have too many naval activities to be as enjoyable as was Boston for liberty but the brief liberty that was granted the first day was a welcome one. The next morning we were informed that we were to accompany the *Alaska* on a post shakedown cruise, which was to last approximately one week. So once again it was anchors aweigh.

A week of intensive drills were conducted and the slight flaws noticeable were remedied. It was on the west coast that we were able to conduct a concentrated shore bombardment. It was not new to us and it was a drop in the bucket compared to what we would experience in the future. Yet we did manage to have a few normal liberties that were enjoyable and well earned.

Scuttlebutt was by this time rampart throughout the ship. A number of our type ships were forming at Pearl Harbor, we were going directly to Saipan, we were expected in Australia. But all this scuttlebutt had no grounds, everyone knew it and it was taken lightly.

Our orders were soon in coming and the word was passed to all hands that we were top escort to troop transports to Pearl Harbor. We were not alone in the task for assistance would be rendered by the *Shannon* DM-25 and the *Bauer* DM-26. The three of us were all in the same division and this was our first assignment where we would work together as a unit.

OUR DESTINATION IS PEARL HARBOR :

" Man your special sea details ", these were the words that rang throughout the ship late in the afternoon of the nineteenth of December. It meant that we were getting underway and that we would soon be hoisting up the anchor. This time there was a deep significance attached to these business like words, for we were leaving the sanctuary of the harbor and proceeding out into the combat areas. If you were to drop in on us now, then you would see the wistful eyes that strained in their anxiety to obtain a fleeting glimpse of the coast line of our native land. We all knew that a great deal of time would elapse before we would again view this enjoyable sight.

A submarine passed us on the port side and she was travelling along at a rapid pace. She was like a veteran returning triumphantly home, an experienced ship with a joyous crew waiting to touch their native soil. It did not take much imagination to assume that it was old meeting new. An old experienced veteran who had taken her trails and tribulations in stride. A veteran who had seen and experienced the horrors of modern warfare. It was we who had passed her with the ambition, vitality and aggressiveness of youth. Yes, we danced across the water and we wheeled

16

and darted to show how impressive we were. Why, were we not the latest threat the Navy had ? It surely must be admitted that we were courageous. Why ; were going out and finish up this war in short order. This veteran stared at us in an understanding way and acknowledged our antics with a sincere expression of good luck.

The trip was quite smooth and uneventful. We made a smart trio as we screened our charges with the dexterity that is obtained only by experience. It demonstrated that we three would click as a unit.

The one constructive aspect of the trip was the close knit cooperation we developed with each other and the knowledge that we were in the company of dependable companions. We were closely bond, we three, by a spirit of comradeship. An example of such, is evident in the following Christmas greeting that we received.

TO : BELLIGERENT BAUER & FEARLESS FRASER :

In accordance with the following wishes promulgated.
A paucity of sixty degree rolls, phantom pips, dope offs,
reciprocal bearings, cloud covered skies and inoperative
bogies. A cornucopia of rubber mine padeyes, smooth sailing,
good luck and good hunting. It is further directed that a
quick and permanent chastisement by this unit of those
blankety blank yellow bellied (with the help of the other
fellows on our side) be affected. Finally heres wishing you a
speedy return to home and fireside. In other words to all
hands a VERY MERRY CHRISTMAS !

SASSY SHANNON

PEARL HARBOR :

" So this is Pearl Harbor, the great naval base in fair Hawaii." Yes it was an impressive sight and the terrible disaster that befell it on that fateful December seventh was still in evidence as a convicting and convincing illumination as to the reality, treachery, cunning and ruthlessness of the Japanese enemy. Yet , it was insignificant under the shadow of the tremendous construction of military projects that have sprung up since that black Sunday. The beautiful green scenery and the rugged, rolling hills provided a contrasting background to the naval anchorage and the military might that was predominant in this past playground of the world.

It was one month that we spent in the Hawaiian Islands and the time sped quickly by. Here we established contact with the *Smith* DM-23 and so the division was complete. We all became closely acquainted and remarkably attached to each other during our training operations as a unit. During this training we assisted in amphibious operations, in shore bombardment and we also did some practice mine laying. We had at this time, an opportunity to observe the forming of the other divisions in our squadron but we were very self centered and could see nothing but our own unit.

Our time at Pearl Harbor was fairly pleasant. We were permitted to enjoy regular liberty hours and we all went in to Honolulu or Waikiki Beach at one time or another. We found the prominent areas to be intensely congested with service men and the transportation system was so badly over taxed that after two or three liberties we were satisfied to stay at the Naval Base and enjoy its meager facilities.

From our vantage point at the destroyer base, the increased tempo of the war was very evident due to the occasional arrival of badly damaged or crippled ships, many of which were hit by bombs, aerial torpedoes or the growing menace of suicide planes. To see a ship with one of her gun mounts or stacks completely blown off or to be minus a bow or stern was not too startling. This is just what we would have to contend with in the very near future.

It was while we were observing this damage wrought and discussing the increased tempo of the war, that time crept up on us. Before we all could completely grasp the situation we had hoisted anchor and were off into the forward areas.

A STOP AT JOHNSTON ISLAND :

It was the twenty seventh of January when we left Hawaii, it was just a month and a day to the day that we had arrived. Perhaps at this time the crews impression of their ship should be brought forth because it was at this time very pronounced.

The crew had been driven hard, of this there was no doubt. The men dubbed the ship the " Turn To, G.Q. Fraser " and this was by far one of the more polite names. It was the Captain's policy to make the training as tough as possible and also to keep a tight rein on every man. Unfortunately there was no conclusion to our strict training curriculum after we left Bermuda. The Captain was merciless in this respect although he was lenient in a few minor details. A few samples of his policy were to keep the men strapped to and stand up at their guns for five hours at a stretch in the areas where air attacks were not possible. All men at the topside watches had to wear the heavy helmets at all times and this proved to be unbearable. At every opportunity and for no apparent reason general quarters would be sounded. If we did finally have a breathing spell then the word would be passed through the public address system " Turn to, Clean up Ship. "

This time as we left Hawaii we had a large number of transports loaded with veteran Marines with us. It was quite obvious that our squadron was well represented for we noticed a number of light minelayers acting as escorts and our division of four were all in on it. Our first stop was to Eniwetok in the Marshall Island but after two days out we were sent on a special mission to Johnston Island about three hundred miles from our estimated position. We arrived there the following morning and our stop was brief. They sent out a motor launch for we anchored out about three miles. We did have an opportunity to observe a few of the details. The island was small and had an elevation of approximately twenty feet above the water. It was quite bare of trees and had a large number of military establishments. Apparently they had a fair sized airfield for we observed the large land based search aircraft take off and land there. We had been there about an hour before we departed. It was the following day that we rejoined our task unit.

THE MARSHALS :

It was the day that we rejoined the convoy that we crossed the International Date Line, the time was in the vicinity of 2 PM and it was the last day of January. To many of us it meant a great deal for we had never been so far away from home before and yet to others it was just crossing the old dateline again. Generally some sort of initiation was in store for the new men before they could enter into the mythical Order of the Golden Dragons. This time it was just an object for discussion and keeping in line with wartime customs. However each man did receive a card that proclaimed the bearer to be a member of the Order of the Golden Dragons for having crossed the international dateline.

The trip was pleasant though slightly tense for we knew that sometime in the near future we would assist in the invasion that was definitely coming. The third of February found us sailing serenely along and basking in the hot sun whenever permissible. At this time we were just 350 miles from Jap held island of Wake. We learned through unofficial channels that the Japs had announced the approach of our force. We knew, however, that we had not been spotted for we were always on the alert for enemy reconnaissance planes that might come from any of the small Jap held islands that had been passed by MacArthur.

It was the seventh of February that we arrived at Eniwetok and anchored in a large lagoon. The islands were numerous, bleached and sandy comparable to Johnston Island in elevation although they did have more vegetation even in view of the fact that they underwent heavy shell fire during their conquest. The natives were friendly and were allowed to sail around in small sail boats providing of course that they kept a respectable distance from the men of war.

It was here that we refueled and took on supplies and we were once again primed to go. The

Navy's mail service proved itself very efficient by having delivered a large quantity of mail from Pearl Harbor by air and the crew enjoyed an unexpected mail call.

Eniwetok was just an interlude on our trip to Saipan. A sort of pause that refreshes and so, refreshed we once again were underway.

SAIPAN :

It was the eleventh of February that we arrived at Saipan one of our latest conquests from the Japanese. The trip from the Marshall Island to this stronghold in the Marianna Chain was very quite and the scuttlebutt now was that we were to invade Iwo Jima in the Volcano Islands a scant six hundred and seventy miles from Japan.

The destroyers and light minelayers received no easy berth at the Saipan anchorage, as did the cruisers and battlewagons, for there was a threat of submarines. The anchorage at Saipan being very wide and open to the sea was the answer to a submarine's prayer and particularly so in the absence of submarine nets. So the destroyers and ships of our class were sent out to provide two anti-submarine screens, one inside the other. In the event the submarine was able to pierce the outer screen without detection she would still have to contend with the inner screen. We were out on this duty all during our stay at Saipan and apparently the job was well done for no enemy submarine activity was reported.

Here at Saipan the majority of us had our first glimpse of the Superfortress. Saipan being their large Marianna base they were always around. Great fleets of them would leave in the wee hours of the morning and they would straggle back all during the afternoon. They were tremendous planes to observe in the air and we were certainly glad they were on our side.

It must have been tough on the Marines for they had been on those troop ships for more than two weeks without having their feet on solid ground and they are not used to confined spaces over so long a period. We knew that when they did get off the beach would not be waiting to give them anything but hell.

It was at Saipan that we went through maneuvers similar to those that we would conduct when we were at Iwo Jima. It was necessary that each man know his job to perfection. It was the fourteenth of February that after having completed maneuvers and having taken on fuel and supplies we departed. Our next stop was IWO JIMA !

THE TRIP TO IWO JIMA :

" War is a Grim Business " , no words were more truly spoken and it was quite evident amongst the crew. The carefree attitude was gone and every man was fully alerted. On the off hours from their watches they labored over the sheath knives until they were razor sharp. the gunners mates toiled for hours upon the guns assigned to them and they were reluctant to leave them until the intricate mechanisms were functioning smoothly and with perfection. Every man wanted to have his equipment in perfect condition and he was not satisfied until it performed better than it ever did. We know that when we met the enemy we would be fully capable of dealing with him.

The Captain informed us as to the danger of our task and each man received instructions on what to do and say if captured by the enemy. We also had plane recognition and first aid instruction both of these would prove beneficial. Our unit was about vessels but there were other such units of about the same size heading toward that tiny island. We had an idea that the Japanese knew of our departure from Saipan but our course was so irregular that it is doubtful if they know where we are. A number of times we located a large number of planes in our vicinity but they always turned out to be superforts on the deadly business of making rubble out of Japan.

All during our approach to Iwo Jima the heavy units of our fleet had been bombarding it unmercifully and it had been bombed by our aircraft consistently for over a month. Therefore the Japs knew that the invasion would be forth coming. The nineteenth was to be the day of the invasion and the trip from Saipan was only five days in duration. By the eighteenth the signs of nervousness began to show and late that night when occasional flashes illuminated the far off horizon faintly it was an indication that the end of the trip was near at hand and that we would face the enemy in the morning. Many of us had a restless night and sleep was difficult in coming.

ACTION WITH THE ENEMY :

It is now early morning on the nineteenth of February. The spontaneous flashes of brilliant flame on the horizon of this dark early morning confirm to us the presence of our enemy and the persistence of our naval forces in attempting to soften him up for the amphibious operations that are to commence within the next three hours. Battle stations are manned instantly upon the setting of general quarters and each man had an opportunity of obtaining coffee before the setting of general quarters.

By now we have detached from the troop transport group and the ships of our squadron proceeded in close to the beach abreast of each other. Our orders are to search out and destroy enemy submarines, mines and other hazards that might impede the coming operation. The air of nonchalance can no longer be displayed about and there is an uneasiness about the whole crew. There are three of us at stations within the sonar hut and we are all business. It was just a few minutes ago that we admitted to each other that we were scared.

It was quite dark in the sonar room and exceptionally quite except for the monotonous, relentless singing of the sound equipment. By the eerie light of the sound equipment I can make out the tenseness of my fellow soundmen's faces and I know that mine also is set in a hard cast. With a quickening pulse of the engines we start in. Everyone of us fully alerted watching, scanning and intensely listening for the danger that must surely lurk there. Closer and closer we approach this tiny island and the large ships further out put up a deafening barrage.

Many thoughts are running through our minds. Have we written home recently, is our life jacket securely fastened, is the island on our port or starboard side and the resolutions that we make to correct our sinful ways are numerous.

So far so good, no trouble as yet. We have to contend with the dreadful shore batteries that can reach us for we are in very close. Any moment we expect to hear the shells come thudding through our thin bulkheads. We have to allow this enemy the tremendous advantage of firing first and then we must act with haste in locating their gun battery and silencing it with our guns before it can destroy us.

Then before we know it we are out again. In and out ! What a joy ! We have carried out our first operation. Apparently the big ships out there on the horizon silhouetted against the rising sun and looking so formidable have done a thorough job in silencing the Japanese batteries. Their job has been well done.

A CHANGE IN OUR DISPOSITION:

We were informed that our Marines had made a successful landing on the volcanic ash that constituted the beach, but we ourselves had no way of knowing for immediately after we had made that sweep in close to the island, we hustled out to our predetermined patrol area. This area was unquestionably at least five miles out from the island and our duty was to detect all surface, air and undersea craft that might attempt to attack our forces that were in closer to the beach.

The Captain secured the battle conditions with a warning to all hands that they must refrain from sight seeing, for there was plenty of danger from stray shells. Since the greater majority of us were new to action we paid no heed to his warning and whenever the opportunity presented itself we would gaze at the momentous struggle that was being conducted. Occasionally a geyser of water would shoot skyward to keep us informed that the Captain's warning was not to be taken lightly but none of these were anywhere close to us. The story is going around the ship at this time was that one of our cruisers was damaged badly in retaliation while bombarding the island defenders three days previous to the amphibious landing and during the time that the large units of the fleet were softening up the defenders of this tiny island.

Many of the men were disappointed in our assignment, regardless as to how vital it was, for they wanted to get in a blow at the enemy and be able to see some of the terrible destruction that surely must be wrought upon the beach. But we all contented ourselves by keeping as sharp a lookout as was possible, but the rest of the morning remained uneventful.

At 1430 we were ordered in to assist in bombarding enemy installations, so apparently the Marines were having a difficult time in subduing the enemy. The whole operation was supposed to take three days to complete. A ship pulled away from the immediate area of the beach and came out to relieve us. It was a destroyer and it was obvious that they were glad to obtain a quite patrol station. We likewise were glad to be able to get in to do our share and we churned the water in our anxiety to fill the hole in the firing line. We fell into place and waited our orders and once again all hands were at battle stations.

A DAY AND NIGHT OF BOMBARDMENT :

After a short wait one of the numerous shore fire control parties contacted us on voice radio and gave us our first target, its bearing and its range. Promptly our guns trained on the target and a full salvo went whistling towards its destination. Immediately necessary corrections to our aim were relayed to us from the beach and with this necessary information the corrections were made and the next salvo was dropped right on the enemy installation.

this procedure was repeated on other targets with the same drastic results. The information from the shore party proved to be necessary and vital, for the target in most cases was obscured to us. We did not locate our own targets, for the shore fire control party knew where our fire support would be most beneficial. A few times a situation arose where our support was needed immediately to stop the slaughter of our valiant Marines who were momentarily cut off from reinforcements and we turned to this task with haste and unerring accuracy. Our fire was generally directed at pill boxes, block houses, machine gun nests and caves where the stubborn resistance of our enemy impeded our advance.

It has been generally agreed that we knocked out thirteen pill boxes that afternoon and the targets were so numerous that the time between the destruction of one target and the locating of another was negligible. We were informed from the beach that our firing was extremely accurate and from that time forth we were in demand.

Towering above everything, on the southern end of the island, was a large volcanic crater and known geographically as Mount Surabachi. To the men engaged in this operation it was know as " Hot Rocks " and this name is more appropriate not because the ash that comprised the slopes was very warm but rather that the Mount was bitterly contested. We had an opportunity late in the evening of the first day to come in very close to " Hot Rocks " and a vivid picture of the struggle there, was firmly implanted in our minds.

We could clearly see the Marines as they dug in to hold the territory they had taken for the day, for the Japanese tactics are to infiltrate our lines during the night. Some of our units were attempting to push ahead a little further and enemy machine guns would throw them back. Occasionally one of our own men would fall and at the first opportunity he was carried to the rear. To climb the slopes of " Hot Rocks " was to risk almost certain death and yet our men were doing just this, in spite of heavy enemy fire. The whole Mount was catacombed with caves, each one from the smallest to the largest was heavily defended by fanatical Japanese.

Though night fell upon us quickly the tempo of the battle did not decrease, and our men continued to kill an to a lesser extent, be killed. We received orders to proceed to a certain sector off the beach to fire star shells and therefore illuminate enemy positions. We all were still at battle stations and no man had strayed from his gun since 1400. From this point off shore we continued to illuminate the enemy all night. The glow of the flame throwers was plainly seen as the Marines continued to clear out pill boxes and caves.

During the latter part of the night and into the early part of the morning we were ordered to fire star shells rapidly and constantly, great haste was essential and we carried out these orders to the best of our ability. When morning finally arrived , we were all bleary eyed and weary, for we had been alerted and at battle stations since the previous afternoon. Since no let up was in sight we were all issued emergency field rations, and this constituted a meager meal.

We received a message from the beach informing us that due to our illumination and firing an enemy counter attack had been detected and successfully repulsed. They furthermore stated that our illumination that night had been extremely accurate and the finest they had witnessed and that our vital role was greatly appreciated. You may be sure that many a tired weary head was lifted, many an eye began to sparkle with a new found vigor.

A BREATHING SPELL :

We were relieved that morning and we retired to the sanctuary of the screening stations to lick our wounds. No, the enemy had not inflicted damage upon us, for his mortars could not reach out to where we had been stationed. Our own guns were the chief offenders for the constant firing and terrific concussion were bound to have a strong effect on the ship's structure.

Just about all the electric light bulbs were smashed, every article that was loose or insecurely fastened was battered down to the deck. All welding that had not made tight unions had torn apart. Valves that were originally secured tightly had eventually leaked and the water was on the deck of the compartments. Empty powder cases were thrown everywhere and the ship in general had been well shaken up, but we had performed our job well. The men disregarded the confusion and climbed into their bunks for much needed rest. The damage was really negligible and looked much worse than it really was. After all hands began to clean up the ship the job was done in a brief period of time.

The one significant thing about this battle was the air power, for we had numerous escort carriers and the navy pilots contributed all the air coverage and support for the infantry. The only planes the enemy had were burned hulks that cluttered the decimated air strip that up to this time was still in enemy hands.

By now there were many of our armored mobile units and a few of our landing craft battered and burning on the assault beach. Our naval units continued to pour heavy fire into the island until it seemed as if nothing could be left alive due to our savage onslaught. Up to this time we had not been able to see one enemy soldier for they were too well dug in. Even in their rear areas the enemy had no mass troop movement. They were dug in and waiting for us to come after them. Well their wish would be fulfilled.

JUST SIX MONTHS IN COMMISSION :

We were ordered in to relieve one of the fire support ships and much to our surprise we found it to be the cruiser *Vicksburg* CL-86. Apparently the fire control party on the beach thought very highly of us for they were expecting us to keep up the work that one of the Navy's finest cruisers had been performing. So, in we went for a short period of very necessary fire support.

That evening we went to dusk alert and shortly thereafter enemy aircraft were reported in the area and all the men were at once fully alerted. A short while later anti-aircraft fire was noticed on the horizon and we knew that a small cruiser was out there, it was a segment of the powerful task force " Fifty Eight " that had just dealt Tokyo a devastating blow. The Japs were infuriated at our bold attack and this no doubt was the reason the small force out there was under attack when the enemy could have found better and easier targets in our vicinity.

The anti-aircraft fire became more intense until it appeared as if they were throwing up a solid sheet of flame. There was no doubt that our force was under heavy concentrated attack. The action lasted less then five minutes and what enemy planes were still intact were driven off and the protective mantle of darkness once again settled down around us. But under the cover of darkness our small patrol craft were speeding to the scene of the brief action, for disaster had struck out there. One of our carriers had been sunk and there were men in the water to be saved.

In the space of the past few minutes many men had given up their lives valiantly at their battle stations. There were hundreds of men in the water waiting to be picked up and every rescue craft available was out there in an attempt to reach all that were struggling in the water.

At 0330 we were summoned hastily from troubled sleep to our battle stations by a combination of the clanging of the " General Quarters " gong and an authoritative voice over the battle announcing system. The Japs were in again for a light attack upon the immediate area of Iwo Jima. It was ten minutes after four when they had departed and we secured from general quarters.

This was the twenty second of February and we were in commission six months during which time we had traveled twenty two thousand miles.

OLD GLORY FLIES FROM HOT ROCKS :

The twenty third of February was a fairly nice day in spite of the war and we were almost feeling contented. The most dangerous thing that we had to worry about was other fire support ships. The island was very narrow and it was less than eight miles in length. A ring of ships ranging in size from small amphibious rocket launching craft to large powerful cruisers were strung around the island, and they were pouring withering fire into the enemy's positions. Occasionally a ship that was firing to the further side of the island would fire a wild salvo that straddled the ships on the other side, in other words it was easy to fire completely over the island and into your own ships on the other side.

We were straddled once or twice by the guns of our ships but we were also straddled occasionally by ineffective enemy mortar when we came in to close to the beach. The enemy was using large rocket bombs and both the rockets and the mortar positions were difficult to locate because they have a high trajectory and because of the simplicity of their firing of launching mechanism.

At 1030 word was passed over the battle announcing system that the Marines had reached the top of Mt. Suribachi and that " Old Glory " was flying from the summit. By straining our eyes a little bit we not only could distinguish the flag flying but also the small band of Marines that were protecting the site. It had taken them four days to reach the summit and it was four days of bloody fighting, but we would not lose it now that we had it. The operation was supposed to be over three days after it started, but the battle was still in progress on the fourth day and the end was not in site. Iwo Jima was the toughest battle the Marines had fought as yet and our casualties were high. The enemy was resisting with their fanatical defense in which they would eventually commit suicide when they found no escape. At dusk alert that night the Japs came over in their aircraft again. We had reached a point where we would expect them at dusk and again at 0230 and they came over at these times with clock like regularity. There was never an element of surprise gained in their attack for we were always expecting them. That evening at 0230 an enemy plane came close enough to us for us to fire on him, but he stayed out at a respectable distance and neither of us did the other any damage.

THE FIGHT GOES ON :

The regularity with which we would bombard the beach the first day, load ammunition the second day, and go on patrol the third day only to once again bombard the beach on the following, rapidly became a monotonous, tiring and routine cycle. To bombard the island with all of our men at battle stations became impractical, for the men would obtain but a few hours of sleep and so we followed the example of many of the other fire support vessels by firing on condition watches. For under these conditions only one third of the crew would have to stay up.

We found it necessary on many occasions to stay at battle stations the whole night when concentrated illumination was imperative to our forces on the beach. The Japanese were resisting bitterly and every yard we gained was bitterly contested. The opposition encountered by the naval vessels was close to zero and our only danger, when bombarding the helpless enemy, was in closing in less than 1500 yards.

The real thrill during the operation was to watch our naval aircraft attack enemy installations and concentrations. We had no army aircraft here at all and the naval air corps had to soften up the defenses.

In they would come, in a group of four or six, and they would dive down on their objectives with all machine guns chattering. Then with a roar, 2, 4, or 6 rockets would be launched from the wings and they would go through this procedure and would pull out at tree top height. Occasionally feeble anti-aircraft fire would be encountered, but I only saw one plane downed this way.

These carrier planes often would drop an object that appeared to be a large cylinder. When this object would hit, it would spread out in an intense fire that would burn for a long period of time. It was obvious that this was a very superior weapon and by observing its effect a person could tell that the heat generated was tremendous.

THERE IS NO TIME TO BE CARELESS :

One morning we were ordered in for fire support and upon arriving at the designated area we found a number of destroyers lined up about one thousand yards off the beach. Each destroyer had it's fantail pointed toward the beach and when we fell into our assigned station and assumed a position similar to the rest of the ships we all resembled a neat row of army field artillery.

The enemy had been pushed back by this time to the high plateau on the northern end of the island and here they were resisting doggedly. This time we were in close to the island ad since we were not at battle stations, I decided to go out on the boat deck and glance at the conflict. A radar man and I were standing under a forty millimeter platform and talking about the progress of the war. All of a sudden we heard a slap over our heads and then something skimmed close by and hit the main deck with a thud.

We were stunned for a moment but we reached the safety of an inside passageway. Apparently a Jap sniper with good eyesight fired upon us and glanced off only to miss us by a few inches as it passed us by to expend its energy on the main deck about seven feet below us. A short while later the radar man located the bullet on the main deck and with this bit of evidence our tale became authentic. You may be sure, however, that there were two men on board who became exceedingly shy of the fresh air of the boat deck.

There was another time when three of our men were wearing battle helmets and sitting together on the main deck on the starboard side of the ship. Suddenly a machine gun stitched the water on the starboard side and some of the bullets rattled upon the deck, the machine gun must have been well concealed in the caves on the island. We all glanced quickly to see how these men fared and all we found was the three helmets laying side by side. The men had scrambled to the protection of below deck spaces and in their anxiety to get away they discarded their helmets.

THE MARINES USE MORTARS :

To observe the saturation mortar fire of the Marine Corps, a person could readily see the destructive effect of this method. A small area would be chosen as the designated target and every available mortar would be concentrated on it. The firing would last about five minutes and every square foot of that area would be under fire. It is extremely difficult to realize that a Japanese could live through a barrage like that and yet they were so well dug in that they could withstand it and still hold the Marines at bay.

Many a cave was sealed up with Japs inside due to the fire of powerful forty millimeter machine guns mounted on amphibious craft. The rocket barrages of this type of craft were also an impressive sight. They would close in to the beach and launch rockets fifty or more at a time. They would leave the ship with a roar and appear as a solid sheet of flame.

Two destroyers were hit and slightly damaged in our vicinity during the operation. They were the USS *Terry* DD-513 and the USS *Colhoun* DD801. One was hit by enemy mortar fire and the other by a wild salvo from one of our cruisers on the other side of the island. On another occasion in the early phase of the battle we picked up an amphibious tank with a couple of Marines on board. Apparently they had been lost all night for they were approximately ten miles out from the island. After these weary boys had an opportunity to take a shower and have some breakfast we sent them over to another ship for we were ordered in for fire support.

Once while on patrol we located a body floating in the water. We pulled alongside and hauled it aboard. We could tell by the uniform that it was Japanese, it was impossible to recognize the features for the body was decapitated. We examined it for identification but there was none and then we weighted it down and let it sink. This unpleasant sight was the only Japanese we saw during the whole operation.

OUR LAST DAYS AT IWO :

On the eighth of March we were ordered to proceed to Ulithi in the Caroline Islands for the navy's participation in the conquest of Iwo was completed and consequently no longer needed. Up until our last day at Iwo we continued in that vicious cycle of shore bombard, load ammunition and patrol stations. We had carried out our part exceptionally well and we had taken a large toll of the enemy. We went into the operations inexperienced rookies and came out battle-wise veterans.

For an island that was so vital to the defense of the Japanese homeland, the enemy on the island put up a determined and fanatical defense, but the attempts of the Japanese to reinforce or assist their fighting men was practically nil. The vaunted enemy airforce made a poor showing during the whole operation and their attacks may be described as nuisance raids. We will never know why they did not strike back, perhaps it was partly due to our illusive naval task forces operating off their homeland and harassing them with its fighter aircraft. But it was true they made a poor showing and we certainly took advantage of it.

We were lighthearted the evening that we left, for our participation was successful and we had suffered no casualties. We had a good ship and a good crew and a battle-wise Captain.

During our last few days at Iwo we were assigned to a task force which comprised two cruisers and a number of destroyers. The other light minelayers had at that time already left Iwo and were enjoying a rest in Ulithi. Our duty with this task force was to intercept any surface units that might approach from the Japanese homeland and to make a torpedo attack if necessary upon the enemy vessels. We would have found this difficult to do because we did not have torpedoes or torpedo tubes.

When the task force commander realized that we had no tubes for a torpedo attack and when it became necessary to escort some vessels to Ulithi then we were detached from the unit.

ULITHI! :

Our trip was uneventful and we arrived on eleven March. It was a beautiful spot in the Caroline Islands and consisted of a deep blue lagoon surrounded by tiny tropical islands and protected from enemy submarine penetration by treacherous coral reefs. Anchored in this perfect sanctuary was well over two hundred vessels of all the various types that comprise a large modern Navy.

We were assigned to a secluded part of this large lagoon where only mine craft were anchored. Here alone there were over one hundred vessels of specialized types of mine craft. There were small mine sweepers and the large ocean mine sweepers. Along with these were high speed sweepers of a Destroyer type. Also to be found in this category were tiny craft of sub chaser size that were used for destruction of mines brought to the surface. For mine layers, well, there was the rest of our squadron, all powerful-looking ships and there was a number of converted destroyers of world war one type. There was also the large mine layers that were capable of carrying one thousand mines and also we were among outstanding men.

It is truly odd how war affects men, everyone of us were on the railing waving to strangers on some of the other DM's as if they had been life time friends. We were all glad to see the familiar outlines of our type of ship and to enjoy talking to men who shared our trials and tribulations and who have done the same type of duty as we. Many of us made very staunch friends that day.

We were able to reach some of the Navy tenders that were anchored within the immediate area and here we thought we would be able to obtain articles that made a ship manageable, habitable and comfortable. But we ere taken back a bit. Upon encountering the red tape that is common to a number of these vessels. We were informed none too gently that they catered to combat vessels only and they made patronization difficult. We were aggravated by their attitude and we were able to obtain only essential items. For some unknown reason we thought that we were here for a rest and recreation and it was not long before we began to realize what a mistake we had made. Immediately upon anchoring all hands were turned-to on painting the ship.

As for rest from the strains of combat, well, this was not accomplished either. The first night we were there, we underwent an air raid and one of the carriers was severely damaged. After all Ship's work was accomplished, along came barges of stores, ammunition and fuel. So again all hands turned-to on these back breaking assignments and by the time that we had everything finished and the ship was primed for action, we were informed that another operation was to be conducted immediately, so once again it was " no rest for the weary ".

A BEER PARTY :

During our stay at Ulithi we all had an opportunity to go ashore on a beer party. A patrol craft was ordered by the commander of mine forces to transport the liberty parties from the anchored vessels to the site of the party on an uninhabited and Navy supervised island.

The patrol craft came alongside, picked up our liberty party and started in toward the beach. The uniform was dungarees for there was no need of a neat uniform in the tropical underbrush. The island was small and had two boat landings. We headed for one, landed, and then were directed to the enlisted mens recreation area which contained all of the island except for a small well kept area that was designated as the officer's country.

Each man had six cans of cold beer and sandwiches of cheese and Vienna sausage. Many of the men were swimming, collecting sea shells or examining the island, particularly the coral rock formations. others indulged in competitive drinking or gambling, gambling was strong temptation and these men brought their own roulette wheels and other professional gambling devices.

The island was really beautiful and was covered with coconut trees and tropical vegetation. The beach was covered with fine sand but much of the bottom was covered with coral which would cut a swimmer's feet to pieces if he was not careful. After the inactivity of shipboard life under crowded conditions, the men had a tendency to expend a great deal of energy in romping about, consequently we were all tired, thirsty and hungry when we returned to the confines of our ship.

A PRELUDE TO INVASION :

We, with a number of other DM's departed from Ulithi on the nineteenth of March. Our duties were to escort a large number of mine sweepers and to assist them in their coming operations. We traveled at a speed of nine knots and large swells rolled us continuously, but the ocean calmed down after a few days. During our trip we ran across a Japanese mine and sank it with gunfire. This was about the only one during the whole trip.

Finally the news leaked out that we were to participate in the invasion of OKINAWA. We were also informed that Iwo Jima was just a dress rehearsal, a prelude of coming attractions when compared to coming operations. With the advent of this cheering news, once again the men began to sharpen their sheath knives and the gunners toiled ceaselessly on their guns until every instrument of warfare was close to perfection.

About two days from our destination we could see a large force of capital ships on the horizon and we learned that they were part of the famed Task Force Fifty Eight that had been giving the Japanese homeland a lot of trouble. We were certainly glad to see these large carriers, cruisers and battleships for we felt too small and helpless to conduct a pre-invasion sweep all by ourselves. Yet that is exactly what we were to do except for carrier air support. This task force did not remain in the vicinity very long for they did not wish to give away our as yet undetected presence. They knew that they were eagerly sought after, by the Japs, so they disappeared as quickly as they had come into view and we were left very much alone.

We were notified that we were to sweep through a small group of islands know as Kerama Retto, a distance of twenty miles from Okinawa, on the twenty fifth of March and upon completion of this task we would proceed up to Okinawa to sweep along the coast. It all added up to the fact that we were to commence our operation against this powerful Japanese base seven days prior to the actual invasion (LDAY) and that we would go in as close to the beach as was possible in the search for mines.

The job of the light minelayers was to destroy all mines that were brought to the surface and to protect the small mine sweepers against air attack. So we steamed toward Kerama Retto with confidence

IN WE GO :

Action against Kerama Retto was to commence today and the uneasiness of the crew was reminiscent of Iwo Jima. General Quarters was sounded at 0500 and the operation commenced. Each of the DM's was assigned to a number of minesweepers and proceeded individually to previously assigned areas. We were in charge of six sweeps and later we referred to our charges as the six ugly ducklings for they waddled behind us in single file like a mother duck and her little family.

The conventional method for sweeping was for the mine sweeps to line up abreast of each other and proceed at a moderate speed while the supporting vessel follows behind and destroys the mines, but I heard that part of the time we were leading the sweeps.

We all had a better grip on ourselves than when we proceeded in to Iwo Jima., for we were battle tested. Our sweeps went in and after a time we followed behind. The islands were rugged and towering over a hundred feet into the air on each side of us and appear much more insignificant than we were. We were ready to counter with guns should Jap artillery open up on us, for it was known that they had installations on these islands. But at least for the present, we met no opposition.

About 0740 we fired upon installations on one side of the island. All of these islands, as mentioned before towered above the water and the distance between them was from one half to two miles. Our carrier planes came in and began bombing all installations and troop concentrations to be found. They met little or no anti-aircraft fire and we met no opposition during the day.

We remained at General Quarters throughout the day and at 1600 we located and fired upon a sulphur mine and buildings. We blew up the sulphur mine and set fires to the buildings. The Japanese would not obtain sulphur from this mine for a long time to come. At 1700 we secured from General Quarters after a hard days work and we were glad that we received no resistance. The Japs had promised after the Iwo Jima invasion that they would no longer allow mine sweepers to carry out operations unmolested. We couldn't help but wonder why there had been no air opposition but we were not complaining because we had been neglected.

THE SWEEP CONTINUES :

We started the morning of the twenty sixth of March by jumping out of bed and manning our Battle Stations for air alerts at 0215 in the morning and again at 0425, then dawn alert was sounded at 0500 to complete a sleepless night. During these alerts there were no enemy aircraft sighted in the near vicinity, but never-the-less Battle Stations had to be manned. Our carrier aircraft gave the Japs no let up for they continued to bomb everything in sight. Okinawa had been under continuous air attack for two days. The next day was a repetition of the first, starting with air alerts at 0145 in the morning and another at 0330. However, this time we fired at the enemy, but our challenge went unheeded and consequently the results were negative. The system used here for air attacks were flash conditions. Flash red meant enemy aircraft were in the immediate vicinity and flash white was the all clear. A point to be brought out is that when ever flash red is passed all men must man their Battle Stations day or night.

On twenty seven March we had our routine dawn alert at 0525 after a sleepless night and then continued our sweeping operations. We finished our assigned sector without detecting any mines and then proceeded to the assistance of another group of sweeps that were a little slow in covering their area.

At the completion of the sweeping operation at Kerama Retto we proceeded to Okinawa to commence the sweeping assignment there. We assisted in the bombardment of Okinawa and illuminated the target area with star shells that night. The island was very large, about sixty miles in length and ten miles wide at some points. It was obvious that the operation conducted on the Navy's part could not be similar to Iwo Jima, for the area was too large and there is about one hundred thousand Japanese troops to be contended with.

THEY BACK US UP :

The twenty eighth of March was here and we tumbled out of bed for dawn alert. Many of us felt fine for we had more than the two or three hours of sleep that we had obtained on the previous two nights. During the dawn alert the Japs conducted a small air raid but it was of no consequence to us.

We started the day out by going in and sweeping again. The sweeps would travel parallel with the coast and we a bit further out would run parallel with the sweeps. A small number of (PGM's) specialized mine craft were with us and their job was to destroy all mines brought to the surface. Further out than us and also running parallel to us were two battleships and one cruiser. The battleships were not our most modern and consequently could not keep up the pace of our fast task forces but they were battle tested in the Normandy invasion and were supposed to be the best shore bombardment vessels the Navy had.

So, there were three lines of ships moving parallel to the beach and as we reached the limit of our sector, we turned around and traveled back to the opposite limit. Each time we turned we went in closer. The battleships and the cruiser kept up a constant bombardment of the enemy defenses and this no doubt is the reason that we were not bothered by enemy fire. They knew the accuracy of our guns and they were reluctant to open fire from their camouflaged positions for they would give away their location. The closer in we swept, then the closer in the bombardment group came and consequently the larger the area that came under the muzzle of their guns. They would let go a salvo with a roar and we could hear it as it whistled over our ship and thud unto the concrete fortifications that could be observed with a long glass.

As soon as it became dark we would retire from the area as a precautionary measure and the Jap aircraft that always attack at night would have to locate us out in the black of night. Unfortunately for us there was a full moon during this part of the month and it made it a great deal easier for the Japanese pilots to locate us. At 1800, and again at 2300 we had enemy planes close by and flash red was sounded, but neither of these occasions did the Jap airmen locate us.

AMERICAN LIVES ARE LOST :

Activity has been greatly increased by the enemy. The air attacks continue at all hours of the night and the men catch their sleep during the day if at all possible. A lot of us have become reluctant to sleep below, others insist on sleeping at their Battle Stations. The first strains of battle fatigue have begun to show, and yet the invasion has not come off.

Enemy submarine activity has been reported and a few submarines have been believed to be sunk by our destroyers. One of our cruisers has had torpedoes fired at her a few times but so far has been able to detect them quite a distance away and in each case has taken evasion maneuvers. Kerama Retto has become a supply bastion and all sorts of supply vessels are anchored in between the towering land masses. The island offers a natural protection from aircraft. Apparently the Japanese never did realize that we would take Kerama Retto first in preference to Okinawa and consequently emplaced meager defenses. Already Kerama Retto has proved its value to the invasion for a long line of fighting ships are continually arriving and departing from this supply area.

We are still conducting the sweeping operations and the first Japanese mines are being cut up. We destroyed three during this operation. Some just sink, but others are detonated. They explode with a tremendous roar and it is easy to understand how they can sink a ship. They are up to this time the most devastating weapon I have observed. They shoot a geyser of water and shrapnel well over one hundred feet in the air. It is best to fire at them at a distance of about one and a half miles away.

One night as we were retiring from the area we saw one of our most modern destroyers in the vicinity of the sweep mine fields. All of a sudden there was a roar, a sudden brilliant flash and a heavy concentration of smoke around this hopeless vessel. When the smoke cleared away, the destroyer was not in sight and not a ripple was on the water. Only 87 men were saved from the crew of over three hundred . No one knows whether the ship was sunk by a sub or a mine.

CHALK ONE UP FOR TOMMY :

It had been a hard tiring day and the night brought forth a beautiful full moon that illuminated the Philippines Sea to a silvery incandescence. A cool breeze arrived to caress the metal plates of the ship, plates that had become too hot to touch under the intense rays of the sun during hours of daylight. The compartments and our bunks were welcome sights to us all as we threw ourselves on them for the deep sleep that is the only consolation of a weary man. No one bothered to undress, for that was a thing of the past, we did not even bother to take off our shoes. To undress was pure insanity, for we could expect to man our Battle Stations five and six times during the night in this area. To grope in the dark for clothing and shoes was to imperil your life and that of your shipmates and therefore you slept fully clothed with your life jacket near at hand. Now this was condition as we were retiring from the immediate area of Okinawa. (0250) The general alarm!!! With it clanging incessantly in our ears we grabbed our life jackets in the dark and started for the ladder as quickly as possible. Before ten seconds had elapsed the condition watches on the guns were firing continuously and we knew we were being attacked by a plane. " All Hands Man Your Battle Stations on the Double ", that was the word that came over the battle announcing system and though we heard it, it was unnecessary for we were traveling as fast as possible.

Upon reaching the main deck we noticed that the gun mounts were firing to starboard and for us that slept in the after compartments we knew that our best bet was to travel up the port side. That after twin five inch mount would knock us sprawling when it fired, if we were to go up the conventional starboard side. So we raced up the port side on the main deck. We were all bent over double to obtain extra speed and at the same time receive less concussion from our main battery which by now was firing like mad. I watched one man reach the top of the ladder to the boat deck only to be knocked down to the main deck again by the concussion of the five inch gun mount as it began to fire to port, apparently the plane had circled the ship. As I was about to try my luck at the ladder there was a terrific roar as the enemy plane was hit and it burst into a bright orange ball and toppled into the water where it burned fiercely.

" The Old Thomas E. is no longer a virgin ", were the words that were emitted as the whole crew signed with relief. At the time few of the men knew that two more of the enemy were closing in on us but they turned away when they saw the fate of one of their friends. The men had continued to pour lead into the plane even when she hit the water, it was hard for them to realize that the plane was all through. At the time the plane was hit it was only about fifty feet above the surface of the water and it was hit a number of times before it was finally stopped. It is doubtful if one fifth of the crew had been able to man their stations before the plane was destroyed. The plane was a Jap " Betty " as known to the Navy. It is a large twin engined bomber and can carry a torpedo and has a crew of more than four men. The plane is very fast, a very good plane and the best medium type bomber Japan had at that time.

We searched the immediate area for survivors but none were found. This section made us all a little more cautious. From the time they sounded General Quarters until the time the plane was destroyed, less than two minutes had elapsed so it can be readily seen that every second counted. I might add that at this time the crews attitude was changing about the ship and they began to call it the " Old Thomas E. ", an affectionate name for a ship that was only about eight months old.

A VAL IS OURS :

Japanese suicide planes have been appearing frequently of late and as yet no adequate defense has been built up against them. Even though they are hit the momentum carries them on.

Actually they have as yet little success in attacking ships for they are detected long before they reach their target.

We have by now become quite confident of our ability to ward off a moderate attack by aircraft. Our sweeping operations continue with success during the day and at night we retire from the immediate area as quickly as possible. General Quarters continues to be called at all hours of the night and early morning and we all know that the danger is great. There is no doubt about it, this operation is hell. All the men are so weary from the lack of sleep that they can hardly stand their watches.

On March thirty first we had two memorable incidents occur. We went to flash red at 0100 for an enemy plane was approaching. We tracked him for quite a while and it was quite apparent that he did not locate us. Then all of a sudden he saw us silhouetted against the moonlight, so he started in. As soon as he was within six miles, our five inch guns started firing. He was intent on coming in and it was miraculous the way that he flew unharmed through our anti-aircraft fire. The range was closing rapidly and by now the five inch gun mounts were firing frantically for we could not allow him to hit.

Finally he decided the flack was too thick for him and perhaps he wasn't a good kamikaze, anyhow he veered away and when he did he exposed a vulnerable belly. It was a perfect shot and we poured everything we had into his tail, he continued to bank away, but then he faltered in mid air and his wing dipped. He plunged into the water and sank from view. This was the second plane for us , and our enthusiasm knew no bounds. For a short while we forgot how close to death a lot of us had come, in our jubilation. The Jap plane was a " Val ", and it was a Navy dive bomber. We located no survivors in the area. The second incident that night was the most memorable and occurred at 0348.

A CLOSE ONE :

The second memorable occasion that night was not long in coming. After splashing that enemy plane we secured from Battle Stations and once again attempted to obtain some much needed sleep.

" Check unidentified plane on the starboard bow ", came the word from an alert lookout on the condition watch. From " Control " came the very prompt and self assured reply, " Plane is a friendly ". This plane was travelling in a random direction and then quite suddenly it started towards us. It was approaching from dead ahead and the target angle was zero. If this plane were to continue on it's present course it would fly directly over us. Of course the men did not give it too much consideration because " Control " had never mistaken the identity of a plane yet.

The plane continued on in and was flying so low that it just cleared the mast. Although the markings on the plane were not distinguishable it was observed that it was a small pontoon plane. It traveled the length of the ship and just as it cleared, the pilot dropped a bomb and it exploded just off the fantail. It is very fortunate, indeed, that the Japanese airman was intent on fouling up our steering and propelling mechanisms by dropping his bomb on the after end of the ship. Other wise he might have dropped it amidships and with the target offered and the extremely low altitude at which he flew he certainly could not have missed. The ship immediately went to Battle Stations, but element of surprise was the enemy's.

Down below decks men alarmed by the explosion sprang from their bunks. It was generally believed by the majority of us that it was the main battery that fired a salvo, as one of these guns mounts was directly above us. We all knew that we were in immediate danger, by the excitement in the young Quartermaster's voice as he passed the word over the battle announcing system for all hands to " Man your Battle Stations on the double ". As it was , we all slept in a restless sleep since we arrived in this area and consequently we did not have to be told to hasten.

It actually proved fruitless to man Battle Stations because the plane caught us by surprise and he made a quick get-away without even being fired upon. When the initial bearing had been sent to control they mistook it for a friendly aircraft on the same bearing. It is believed that the planes took off from the water in our near vicinity. This may be the first but not the last time a mistaken identity almost cost us our lives.

WE WITNESS A RACE AGAINST DEATH :

We concluded our mine sweeping operations on the thirty first of March and henceforth would be assigned to patrol stations. During our sweeping operations we uncovered a mine field and pulled it up making the area navigable for all the units of the fleet.

April first was Easter Sunday but it also was L day or the invasion day. The Marines landed on the West coast of Okinawa against meager resistance and as the saying goes, " In a few hours they had the situation well in hand ". The day turned out to be a tough one for us because we had air attacks upon the fleet units during the very early part of the morning and again after sunset. We were called to our Battle Stations five times during the day.

At sunset on the day of the invasion we were ordered, along with the other DM's to form an anti-aircraft screen around the troop transports. The vessels were to retire from the immediate area during the night and return in the morning. The reason was to keep these valuable ships from being subjected to the all night air attacks that the Japanese conducted.

We were still a considerable distance away from these transports when the Japanese made their first attack of the evening. A Jap plane appeared out of nowhere and circled the transport unit while every ship in the area tried in vain to knock him down with anti-aircraft fire. The pilot with great deliberateness picked out a large, loaded troop transport and then started down on it in a Kamikaze dive. The gunners of that particular transport really poured on the fire but the plane remained steadfastly on its collision course.

Every man on every ship in the vicinity watched the impending catastrophe with fascination. They all prayed that the guns on that particular transport would find their mark for a great deal of young lives would be lost if the plane crashed into the vessel. Closer and closer the plane came and the more frantic and desperate the guns fired. Just when it looked as if the plane would collide, a five inch projectile found its mark and it literally tore the plane apart. Even the most toughened fighting man cheered like an excited school boy at this fortunate outcome. We finally closed into position and all the transports retired from the area escorted by trim destroyers. The expanse of the Philippines Sea swallowed them up and night covered them with a protective cover of darkness.

WE SPLASH THE THIRD :

The bright moonlight was favorable to the Japanese airmen and they had little trouble in locating us. We had six attacks during the night and early morning by small groups of enemy aircraft. During one such attack we fired over five hundred rounds of five inch projectiles at one plane without sighting or hitting the plane. Our main battery fired so fast and consistent that they sounded like machine guns.

On another occasion we fired on a plane that was four or more miles away. He immediately turned and headed in toward the whole unit. Every ship with us put up a concentrated barrage and yet they could not stop this fanatic. He closed in and placed himself closest to the *Ditter* DM-31 and us. We both fired until the range was too close for the main battery and we reverted to machine guns to knock him down. One of our quad forty millimeter guns had an opportunity to get in a good burst and the men back there on it really poured it on. The plane staggered but righted itself and doggedly kept to its course. It reached the transports but it was so badly damaged that it crashed into the water. The Commander in charge of the unit called the Squadron Commander and informed him of the damage. He further stated that the plane was shot down by either the *Ditter* DM-31 or the *Fraser* DM-24, and left it up to the Squadron Commander to decide as to who should be credited with it. Since the Squadron Commander had witnessed the action from close by, it was quite obvious to him that it was our ship that knocked down the plane. Therefore, credit was given to us, boosting our total to three planes.

OUR DEPARTURE FROM OKINAWA :

We have been having a great deal of trouble with the rotation of our radar antenna and now it has ceased to rotate completely. Though this condition cannot be repaired at sea, it can be remedied at any naval base. It is a real bad predicament to be in at Okinawa because enemy aircraft are next to impossible to detect without the use of radar. We all had hopes that our services could be spared so that we might retire to a rear area base and have effective repairs on this vital piece of equipment.

A few days after the Okinawa invasion we were ordered to make preparations to receive aboard as a passenger Admiral Sharp, Commander of Mine Craft in the Pacific. We took him aboard almost immediately and departed that day enroute to Saipan. There were a number of troop transports and escorts that we travelled with. It certainly was a relief to leave this dangerous area and be able to obtain a full nights sleep. During the previous five days we had been summoned to our Battle Stations more than thirty six times and many of these alerts were for two hours or longer and principally at night. Figuring this in addition to eight hours of watch standing, a person can readily see that sleep was an uncommon occurrence.

We escorted the troop transports for a considerable distance and then we received orders to take Admiral Sharp to Guam rather than Saipan. We proceeded on our new course in the company of the destroyer *Bache* DD-470 at a speed of twenty two knots. Guam came into view at 1400 on April eight. We tied up at the same berth as the *Bache* and Admiral Sharp left the ship almost immediately.

A SAD MESSAGE :

. The personnel attached to the Navy Base at Apra Harbor at Guam wasted no time in repairing all minor damage to the ship. A whole new antenna unit and appropriate accessories replaced our defective equipment and the work was conducted with haste and efficiency. A great deal of fresh stores were brought aboard, much to the satisfaction of the crew.

The facilities to hold beer parties here at this base were excellent and a Navy Fleet Recreation Park had been established just for this purpose. So we all had an opportunity to enjoy a few cans of beer and to indulge in the sports program which comprised two baseball diamonds and a few basketball courts. The Red Cross had set up a fine large building in which coffee and doughnuts were to be had at no obligation. They also had an attractive indoor recreation program but the greatest attraction was the American women who prepared the doughnuts and chatted with the men. At the site for the beer party many men from the ships displayed handmade devices for gambling which were immediately placed into operation and were well patronized. The beer party rapidly took on the appearance of a bazaar. Since the Fleet Recreation Park was over two miles from the dock at which our ship was tied up and because many men had conducted active participation in athletics at the Recreation Park all the men returned to the ship exhausted. The reason for the men to tire so easily was partly responsible to the lack of exercise in many months of sea duty.

The morning following the recreation party we were summoned to division parade and informed that President Roosevelt had died. It was very hard to believe and we all felt just as if some one very close to us had passed away. There was a definite air of humbleness throughout the base and all flags were flown at half mast for many days to come. It was too bad he died before the European war was over, for the end of that phase of the war was in sight.

THE AFTERMATH OF INVASION :

While still undergoing repairs at the dock we observed a long line of ambulances heading in our general direction, probably from one of the hospitals in the interior of Guam. They lined up neatly in the near vicinity of our ship and drivers and attendants began to unload the stretchers. The ambulances continued to drive in until there were over one hundred of them. We cold not understand why they were here unless this medical unit was being shipped to the forward areas via the cargo ships that were anchored and docked near by. If this was the case then why had they taken out the stretchers?

Well we were not long in finding out, for a hospital ship, the USS *Comfort* AH-6 , docked very close to us and having a cargo of wounded veterans of the Okinawa Campaign. The efficiency of the medical department was never more apparent as the stretcher bearers moved forward before the last line was secured. Immediately a gangplank was set up and the stretcher bearers hustled inside. The wounded men were taken off with haste and yet gentle care. The variety of cases was readily observed even from a distance.

There were men swathed in bandages, others unconscious and well wrapped in blankets. There were many amputation cases, both arms and legs and they were pitiful. There were men that were taken off in a sitting position because they were to weak to walk and wounded in places that would not allow them to lie down. Last of all came the walking cases and they were the most numerous of all. Many had been burned and others had been wounded in the arms, a few of these men had minor amputations. In all, they were a pitiful procession as they shuffled off to better care.

Yes, we had been to the very combat area that these men returned from and we had undergone enemy fire, but this was the first opportunity we had of seeing the less fortunate men return from the battle front. If before, we thought there was any glory in war then it was completely discarded now.

OKINAWA BOUND AGAIN :

On April seventeenth we departed from Guam and headed for Saipan, a short distance away. We arrived at Saipan early on the morning of the eighteenth. It was our first time at Saipan, and we were interested in getting ashore. Since the Navy had established a recreation park for the fleet in which beer and coke were rationed, and the maximum was three cans of beer and one coke. The men were not allowed to leave the recreation park but we all had an opportunity to look at a Japanese civilian, for the Navy had some working at the park cleaning up the grounds. They were small, insignificant quiet men and they wore split-toe shoes. More attention was paid to the odd foot gear than to the Jap himself.

They had a locker room at the recreation park at which we left our clothes if we desired to swim. We found the water too warm and too shallow for enjoyable swimming and unstable coral bottom proved both treacherous and hard on the feet. After being in the water five or ten minutes, the men were discouraged and came out. To get into the water deep enough to swim it was necessary to go out about one half of a mile.

We also had an opportunity to examine the intricate Japanese beach fortifications that were not quite good enough. The block houses that the Japanese had built were very strong and the walls were over a foot thick and constructed of reinforced concrete. They had large holes in them however, probably due to the Navy shell fire of explosive charges, for no amount of bombing could be that effective. The camouflage was exceptionally good particularly on their machine gun nests that were aligned along the beach and they also were constructed of concrete. They were covered with sand and cleverly sown plants so that a person would be almost up on top of one before he recognized it. A great deal of men copied or traced the Japanese characters that were imprinted on the equipment found there.

On April twentieth we departed from Saipan, escorting a group of amphibious craft at a base speed of nine knots. Our destination was Okinawa.

A REVIEW OF THE PAST :

It was the twentieth of April that we departed Saipan and because the speed was extremely slow we did not arrive in the Okinawa area until one week later. We first realized we were back in the Okinawa area by being summoned to an air alert.

To review the past and bring to light statistics previously not mentioned : the first DM to be hit by the enemy was the *Adams* DM-27. The *Adams* was hit by a suicide plane that crashed into the after end of the ship and partially disabling her propulsion and steering mechanisms. She tied up beside us during our brief stay at Guam and then she left for Mare Island.

We observed that the *Adams* had six enemy planes to her credit. She was to be laid up for eight or more weeks.

We were very fortunate when we were assigned to deliver Admiral Sharp to Guam and to effect repairs because the day after our departure a large daylight attack was carried out by the Japanese and they hit our naval units at Okinawa very heavy. Up to this time the DM's had done very well. Excluding the score of the *Adams*, there were three of us that had three planes to our credit. The Japanese sent more than three hundred planes over in a daylight attack and the damage they did was considerable. A number of destroyers were sunk and about twenty were damaged. It was definitely known that over two hundred enemy planes were knocked down.

There were so many enemy planes in the air that it was like a night mare for the Navy men. Many a destroyer was attacked by twenty or more planes at a time and this was too much for a small craft as a destroyer. Since the enemy planes were mainly Kamikaze (suicide) planes, it made the raid more terrifying than ever. Nonetheless, the destroyer men gave a good account of themselves. Every destroyer in the area was under attack at one time or another during the day. These men certainly must have been weary, for to stand on your feet behind your guns all day with little or no food and ward off planes intent on crashing into you is definitely no fun. We were glad that we did not have to undergo this attack.

When we returned, all of the DM's had many planes to their credit, but they also suffered many high casualties. The *Tollman* DM-28 was beached on the reefs and they were attempting to get her off. The *Lindsey* DM-32 had sustained heavy damage and casualties due to suicide planes that crashed into her during the large daylite attack and she was on her way back to the " States ". The *Ward* DM-34 had been very badly damaged and was on the verge of sinking for a number of days. She had nineteen enemy planes to her credit. Five suicide planes managed to get through her anti-aircraft fire and they leveled her gun deck almost down to the water line. She suffered many casualties and would have to be towed back to the states. eventually she was placed out of commission. Therefore, out of twelve light minelayers that comprised our squadron, four of them were so badly damaged that they would be out of action for four months or better and the *Ward* looked like a guttered relic that would be placed out of commission. These are the ships that were placed in a non-combatant class !

AN INJUSTICE OBSERVED :

Fueling had just been completed when we received orders to proceed to a designated radar picket station for patrol duty. To all of us on board it was quite obvious that they were in dire need of patrol vessels when they would assign us to picket duty so quickly after our arrival. We proceeded immediately to the sector assigned and relieved a weary crew. They were gratified to be able to return to the sanctuary of Kerama Retto for fuel, ammunition, stores and if luck is with them, some much needed sleep.

We found our station to be a poor station to have for it was very close to land and an enemy plane flying close to the land and very low had a fair chance of approaching to within five miles of us before we could detect him. There was a great deal of activity in this area and within twenty four hours we could understand why the crew of the other ship was so weary. During the twenty four hour period we went to Battle Stations seven times due to enemy air attacks. During one attack at 0300 after we had been assigned to the station a mere eight hours, an enemy plane that had sneaked in quite close before we detected his presence and dropped a stick of bombs very close. They were so close that practically all men on the top side Battle Stations were drenched to the skin by a mountain of salt water that literally covered the ship. We continued to fire but it was to no avail and the enemy was able to get away unharmed. We were very fortunate that this particular enemy was no Kamikaze, for he certainly could have crashed into us.

On the following night the Japanese launched a violent air attack that kept us up the better part of the night. During the height of the engagement word flashed across the voice radio circuit that the USS *Comfort* AH-6 , a hospital ship, was bombed and then crashed by a suicide plane. They apparently suffered heavy casualties for they did not have alert conditions in conforming to the articles of the Geneva Conference.

Word was passed that we, being the closest, were to proceed to her position and render all necessary aid to the stricken vessel. We proceeded at high speed to her position and stood by. Under normal conditions this hospital ship would be brightly illuminated, but in view of the vicious attack all lights were extinguished. Still in all the ship was beautifully outlined against a full moon in a cloudless sky. The *Comfort* informed us that she had the situation under control and requested that we remain for protection against further attacks and to render aid if serious trouble develops.

WE RETURN TO GUAM :

The hospital ship had been severely damaged, of that there was no doubt, and her casualties also were extremely heavy. Her mission was that of mercy work and consequently she was brightly illuminated and the large red crosses that were painted in every conceivable place were very conspicuous. She was not very far from the shore when the treacherous attack occurred and at the time was tending to the wounds of seriously hurt men. The " Kamikaze " plane hit her and penetrated right into the operating room, and in so doing killed a large number of doctors and nurses. The total number killed was over thirty and the number of those wounded was quite high. There could be no case of mistaken identity on the enemy airman's part and he certainly could not miss or be repelled for it is against international law for the hospital ship to carry weapons.

The hospital ship would have to return to a rear area base and since it was desirable that she be escorted, they assigned us this task. So the following day after she was hit, we started back to Guam. This was on 29 April and during the day she was able to restore her communication system and steam at a speed of 14 knots. Her flag was flying at half mast and the gaping holes where the bomb and plane penetrated were covered by canvas. To lend mockery to the incident the canvas was stretching across the damaged side of the vessel and right above the large red cross. On the first of May we had a submarine contact and we made a depth charge attack. In the meantime the hospital ship began to zig zag frantically. We did not regain contact but we continued to search the area for a short while. Because the submarine contact was doubtful from the beginning and because our duty was to stay close to the USS *Comfort*, we discontinued our efforts to locate the underwater target and returned to our normal station near the hospital ship. No further trouble developed and we continued on.

It was the third of May that we arrived at Guam and a few small craft came out and headed our charge to its berth where preparation had been made to take off the wounded. As for us, we headed over to a fuel tanker and filled up our tanks with that necessary fluid. We were ready for come what may.

THEY CALL US BACK :

We stayed at Guam just one day and then we were ordered back to Okinawa. It had appeared that the authorities at Okinawa sent a message to Guam informing the responsible authorities that it was imperative that we be sent back immediately and they made it known that they were indignant because of that one day delay, so it was on this account that we steamed back to Okinawa at twenty two knots. The weather on this return trip was a little rough but not bad enough to slow us down.

At 0230 on may seventh, on the third day of our departure from Guam, we were summoned to our Battle Stations for an air alert, and it was thus we knew of our arrival at Okinawa. At day break we went into refuel and it was during refueling that we received a message welcoming us back and informing us that business had picked up. We also found out, that as happened previously, a very large daylight air attack was launched the day we departed for Guam. Since this was the second time that we missed the large daylight raids that did a great deal of damage, we began to feel as though we were just a " lucky ship ". But these daylight raids on a large scale, though they caused a considerable amount of damage, nevertheless were insignificant in comparison too the numerous long raids on a less spectacular scale that occurred almost every night.

At completion of fueling we were assigned immediately to a radar picket station. The number of ships that were able to do picket duty were very few because of the large number of picket ships hit or sunk on duty. The job of a radar picket ship is to report in advance enemy aircraft that are heading in to attack the island. Since our forces ashore were forewarned by these picket ships operating twenty to fifty miles off the island they were able to inflict heavy damage to the attacking ships. Therefore, the Japanese were attempting to not only eliminate major units of the fleet, but also the mobile radar stations that these vessels played the part of.

WAR IN EUROPE IS OVER :

There were a number of dangerous picket stations that might be had, and one of them was radar picket station fifteen. This station was known as " Bogie Junction ", and bogie is the Navy designation for enemy aircraft. There was also one other station which was to the southwest of Okinawa that was known as " Bogie Junction ", (Radar picket fifteen is northwest of Okinawa and nearer to the enemy home islands). This station to the southwest was the junction point of all enemy aircraft arriving from Formosa, Saki Shima and China, whereas the station to the northwest was the junction point of all enemy planes arriving from Korea, Amami Gunto and the enemy home islands. The heaviest enemy traffic came down from the northwest of Okinawa and was most dangerous. The ships on these stations underwent violent air attacks almost every night. In this action they knocked down an extremely large number of aircraft but generally they ended up by being hit by a bomb, torpedo, or more than likely by a Kamikaze.

Our luck held out, for we were assigned a picket station to the southwest of Okinawa and generally speaking it is as safe as we could ask for of all the picket stations. We were thankful for the next two days of rain and miserable weather for it was this and this alone that kept the enemy on the ground. Another bit of bright news was the announcement that the war is over in Europe. We knew then that half the battle was over and that in the near future reinforcements would be arriving in the Pacific to drive the Japs back to Tokyo. It was gratifying to know that the people back home took V-E day in stride and as for us, well we continued to fight.

With the lifting of the weather the Japs began to arrive again and during the following three days we had eleven air attacks. During one of them, the night of May eleventh, we stayed at Battle Stations from midnight to five in the morning. During all these attacks we only fired once, for only once did an enemy plane come within range. We had wonderful support by our aircraft and especially our fighter planes. In many instances they intercepted large formations of enemy bombers, at night, heading toward Okinawa and these night fighters of ours would splash them all before they reached their objective. Never before had our fighters been more effective.

A TRAGEDY BRINGS TOMMY TWO MORE :

We were relieved at our station at 1700 on May eleventh and we returned to Okinawa for fuel supplies and mail. On the twelfth of May we remained in the harbor and rode at anchor. About 1800 that day everything seemed to happen at once. It had been quiet and peaceful, and the majority of us took advantage of this lull to obtain some much needed rest.

Prior to 1800 there were quite a number of men up on the main deck watching the battleship *New Mexico* BB-40 enter the already crowded harbor and drop anchor near us. Since it was rapidly getting dark the *New Mexico* had her men at Battle Stations for dusk alert. It was quite obvious that she was taking no chances, and then it happened !!

It started with the sudden chatter of machine gun fire as an alert gunner on a nearby ship opened up on an enemy plane that had sneaked in close. On our own ship our forty millimeter crew on condition watch started to fire immediately showing that they were fully alert. It was but a few seconds before every ship had located the enemy and poured out a withering barrage. On board our men were hastily summoned to Battle Stations, but the battle was over before they were fully manned. The actual incident was as follows ;

It appears that two enemy planes had sneaked undetected through our outer defenses and headed in towards the *New Mexico* who had just anchored. An alert gunner on a nearby ship spotted the enemy planes and opened up immediately with his machine gun. Our gunners opened up with their AA guns right away and then every ship in the harbor opened up. The leading plane was definitely a Kamikaze, for he continued on through the concentrated fire even though he had been hit. He had the element of surprise with him and there was little doubt but that he would use it to a good advantage. The *New Mexico*, realizing that she was the main objective, opened up with every available gun but it was to no avail. We were very close to the battleship and it is definitely known that we hit the enemy a number of times, for we were in the most favorable position. Regardless of the amount of flak being thrown at her, the plane crashed head long into the superstructure and exploded with a loud detonation, the burning gasoline spreading far and wide, setting the *New Mexico* on fire.

The second plane met with a luckless fate, for she never did get in close to the battleship. Before she even had an opportunity to suicide we knocked her down into the water where she disappeared readily. It was a sad day for the *New Mexico* for she had suffered very heavily. That Jap plane took more than fifty American lives and caused more than one hundred casualties. A great deal of this high casualty list was due to the fact that the Jap was spraying the superstructure with his machine gun as he came rushing in, and consequently a number of men were killed or injured at the numerous exposed anti-aircraft stations.

After the action had been thoroughly evaluated and investigated, we were given credit for the two Jap planes to bring our total score up to five. We learned that day that there is danger in the harbor as well as the picket stations and that it doesn't pay to relax for one minute.

PERHAPS IT WAS A BAKA BOMB :

Later that night Japanese boats attempted to land men behind the Tenth Army lines right in the harbor but they were quickly destroyed. Again at 0100 we were alerted for an air attack and it was not long in coming. We had an opportunity to fire and the results were negative but then the night was pitch black. We all exclaimed that we would be glad to get back out on picket duty, but we were not long in retracting that statement for we were assigned that morning to a radar picket station to the Northeast of Okinawa.

It was well known that the enemy aircraft had been approaching Okinawa from the Northeast and they had been giving that particular station hell. The Jap planes had damaged and sunk an impressive number of picket ships at that remote but continually traversed station. So, we readied ourselves for heavy action and went out to relieve a harassed destroyer that was very anxious to leave that station. That evening, May thirteenth, we went to Battle Stations at 1930 because of an approaching enemy plane, but the Jap kept a safe distance away and we were not annoyed. The same thing occurred the following night, at the very same time, with the same result. No raids came in from the Northeast but heavy raids came in from the Northwest and gave radar picket station # 15 a very tough time.

It continued this way for a couple of days. This station had been hit heavy every night and now that we take it over we have only one plane during the whole night. On the 16th of May we went to Battle Stations at 0100 and again at 0330. But we did not fire, nor did the *Smith* DM-23 who had joined us that day, for the plane was flying very high. That evening Okinawa was hit very hard by enemy aircraft and they all came in from the west and northwest and though we were alerted a number of times, the night was uneventful. All the time we were subjected to one plane attack.

On the 17th of May we were summoned to Battle Stations due to approaching aircraft. We fired continuously, but he was flying high. During the action our training control for our guns temporarily failed and we fired a salvo into the water from one of our gun mounts. It was fired into the water so close that the men on the port side were showered with flying spray. At the same time a terrific amount of water shot up from out on the starboard beam and drenched all men on the topside Battle Stations. After that we lost track of the enemy plane but every one of us was real mad at getting wet.

It was later that a lot of us began to believe that it must have been a Baka bomb that the plane launched, for that could be responsible for that terrific splash to starboard.

A regular bomb would not have sent so much water on board or strike the water at that angle. Also the enemy plane would have to be almost over us to drop the bomb and we knew that this was not so. It was therefore a logical conclusion that the plane launched a Baka bomb and the pilot of the bomb misjudged his approach and hit the water. But how fortunate for us.

FATE FAVORS THE FRASER :

For the remainder of the night enemy aircraft continued to attack installations at Okinawa and they all approached from the Northwest. On the following day the enemy continued to harass the island and we went to Battle Stations on six different occasions. Fortunately they were not out for blood and we continued to patrol our station without interruptions. At 2030 we were called to Battle Stations because of the numerous air attacks upon the island and the consequent nearness of enemy planes to our position. Two Japanese aircraft teamed up and started simultaneous attacks on us. We opened up with ever available gun that could fire out to their extreme range. As they closed in, they found our flak very accurate. Therefore they turned tail and fled before they came within effective range. The Japs made repeated attacks against the island for the rest of the night and into the early hours of the morning. That was one day in which we were glad to see the sun rise, for enemy aircraft made little attempt to attack during the day because if they did, they were generally knocked down before they came within fifty miles.

That morning we were relieved from our picket station by a destroyer and we proceeded into Kerama Retto which by now we were beginning to call home. Here at Kerama Retto we loaded aboard supplies, ammunition and also refueled. At 0715 we were summoned to Battle Stations once again, for concentrated enemy flights were coming in. The first raid was knocked down completely out of the air by our own fighter interceptors. The striking thing to us about this raid was that the planes all came in from the Northwest, and right at the picket station we had just left. These planes gave our relief hell, and once again we felt as if fate was guiding us along, particularly so in view of the fact that we had been hardly molested all time we were at that dangerous station.

We could hear our relief talking over the voice radio and reporting all the raids. One part of his report went as follows; " Taking a Jap twin engine bomber under fire to port ! " " Taking a Jap plane under fire ahead ! " " Taking a Jap under fire to starboard beam ! " " Oh hell, what's the use of reporting, they are all around us ! " Somehow or another the destroyer remained afloat and was not damaged.

On the afternoon of May 19th we moved over to Hagushi Anchorage at Okinawa and there we took aboard more supplies. It was this day that the Captain spoke and warned us that large scale air attacks by the enemy were eminent. He also warned us of Baka bombs, for they had proven a real menace. That evening we went to dusk alert and heavy air attacks were expected.

WE DRAW A TOUGH STATION :

Since we have received no visits from enemy aircraft that night, we got in some necessary sleep. On the following evening at sunset we had a raid by a small number of enemy planes which have managed to hit a destroyer patrolling on a picket station. After this day the weather turned cloudy, the sea became rough and there was talk of a possible typhoon, which never came. The combination of the weather and the sea were enough to keep the enemy grounded and therefore we caught up on a little more of that lost sleep, providing a person can catch up on lost sleep.

Scuttlebutt was beginning to run wild around the ship now and the indications of another operation was very strong. The weather continued to be bad and no enemy planes ventured into the air. This type of weather is ideal and we should have a peaceful period of time, but we went to Battle Stations on three different occasions because of the presence of aircraft within the immediate vicinity later identified as American planes.

on the twenty third of May we were assigned to a radar picket station to the north of Okinawa and we all realized that this station would prove anything but monotonous. It turned out that we had the toughest and most dangerous station at that particular time and the Japs gave us plenty of trouble, for we were continually in their way on their trip to Okinawa. They did not appreciate our job of announcing their arrival to the military forces at Okinawa.

We relieved the ship on the station and then immediately went to dusk alert. About one hour later the enemy began to arrive. They started out with three raids that approached from the north and northeast. One enemy airman scored a hit on one of the forward picket ships but it did little damage. The enemy continued to attack, and up to midnight they had made seventeen raids. All of these raids came in from the north and northeast which was up in our area. However, they were not interested in us that night, for the closest an enemy plane came to us was eight miles. This night radar picket station # 15 received particular attention from the Japs. Consequently the destroyer on that station knocked down five enemy aircraft, and a destroyer escort in our area downed another. Actually, General Quarters lasted until 0415, but there were two or three intervals between raids that we were allowed to secure.

A CRITICAL NIGHT :

The following night we were patrolling off of Ie Shima, which is a small island to the north of Okinawa. We had an APD which is a converted destroyer escort and used as an attack transport, that tagged along behind us all night. This was done to concentrate fire power and to provide mutual protection. In view of the fact that we had a great deal more fire power than the APD, it was very beneficial on their part to join up with us. Ie Shima had been recently wrested away, and it was on the island that Ernie Pyle had been killed by the Japanese machine gun fire. This was to be the night that we would be subjected to the heaviest air attacks during our stay at Okinawa.

It was 1835 that we were hastily summoned to our Battle Stations due to the approach of enemy aircraft. The Japanese were out to decimate the air field at Ie Shima and we were between the field and them. At first, the attacks were small and infrequent, but were just enough to keep us at General Quarters. At the same time word was received that enemy torpedo boat activity was occurring to the North, but this was rapidly quenched. As time wore on, the air attacks were increased in tempo and some bombs began to hit the airfield.

Apparently the Japanese were informed that they should concentrate only on the airfield and that they should ignore and avoid all other possible targets. This was very fortunate for us, otherwise we would have surely been hit. On only three occasions did enemy planes attack us and get in dangerously close, but they were eventually repulsed. The raids on Ie Shima became so frequent that the field was almost constantly illuminated by anti-aircraft fire and the occasional exploding bombs. The air field personnel did a very fine job of defending the air strip, and combination of search lights and heavy anti-aircraft guns brought down many an enemy bomber. The combat air patrol had the highest score and did the finest job, for the majority of enemy bombers were intercepted and destroyed before they could reach their objective.

As for us and the ships in the immediate area, well, we did our job too. Though the whole night the APD tagged along behind us in our intricate evasive maneuvers and once or twice she fired at hostile aircraft. We fired at any and every plane that came within the range of our guns. There were many enemy aircraft who were to carry some flak from our guns that night. The problem of finding a target was absurd, for it was a question of which of the numerous targets should we track. Most of the night there were so many planes around that we tried to keep on the closest target, and soon as he became discouraged and turned away we would hasten to locate and concentrate on another enemy who was closing in on us. Most of the night was spent thus, switching from one enemy to another whichever was the closest. There were so many enemy aircraft in the air and in our vicinity that the greater majority of the men had already made up their mind that we would be hit that night. We believe now that the thing that pulled us through without getting hit was mainly because we were ignored and could not be classified as even a secondary target. There were a few of the enemy who did not ignore us and when they approached we settled down for heavy attacks, but they turned out to be individual ventures.

These individual ventures were great mistakes on the part of the Jap airmen, and resulted in two more sure kills to our credit. This addition gave us a grand total of seven Japanese aircraft to our credit.

It was after 0500 that we secured. We had been at Battle Stations over ten consecutive hours without a let up in the attacks of more than fifteen minutes. The enemy suffered a terrific loss in planes and they had made over twenty five raids. A large amount of their loss had been due to the work of the picket ships in our vicinity who, like we, had also reported the enemy flights as they were approaching. There was little doubt that the next time they would attempt to eliminate us first.

At 0715 that same morning we were relieved, for we were low on ammunition. We were ordered in to Kerama Retto for fuel, ammunition and supplies and also to have fighter director equipment installed. This equipment would enable us to communicate with and direct a combat air patrol. In this manner we would be a better ship, for we could control a flight of interceptors. When we picked up enemy flights on our radar, we could direct our own planes to intercept and turn back the enemy.

On the return trip to Kerama Retto we went to General Quarters at 0800 for the enemy was approaching. Perhaps in revenge for their unsuccessful night they were going to create some damage and maybe this is the reason they attacked the Ie Shima area. They hit and heavily damaged three ships in that area. One of them was the APD that had followed us around all night and another was the destroyer that relieved us. All this occurred forty five minutes after we had left the station. The Japanese having had their revenge at an additional cost in aircraft, retired from the Okinawa area and the *Thomas E. Fraser* DM-24, a ship of the non-combatant class, anchored in Kerama Retto after an eventful night. For those who pray for us at home we give thanks.

WE BECOME A FIGHTER DIRECTOR :

We were back at our haven, Kerama Retto, and were certainly glad of the small amount of protection that it offered from the fanatical enemy. The weather was very poor with a great deal of rain but it was good for uninterrupted sleep. We loaded ammunition on the day following our arrival and every night during our stay were alerted due to approaching planes. Every ship in the anchorage made smoke, and with the high land masses hemming us in, the smoke clung close to the surface of the water making a highly efficient protective blanket. No ship under the blanket of smoke was allowed to fire at the enemy, unless it was an emergency, for it would give away the position of the ship.

We had a few days availability while we had installed equipment for fighter direction use and these few days kept us off the picket line. The equipment that we received had been previously used on two very unfortunate ships. Both of them had been badly damaged by Kamikaze planes while on picket duty and in view of the fact that they would no longer need the fighter director equipment, it was salvaged and put in a " radio material pool ". We were the second ship to take this salvaged equipment and install it, but we fervently hoped that it would bring us better luck than it did the other two unfortunate vessels. In view of the fact that two other ships had the equipment before us, and both ships were so badly hit that they salvaged the equipment, I made a mental note that under attack it would be advantageous to stay close to this equipment that had survived from two badly damaged destroyers.

On the night of May 27, the ship attempted to benefit the crew with a moving picture but the movie no sooner started when General Quarters was sounded. Enemy aircraft were in the immediate vicinity and we observed anti-aircraft gun flashes. After the raid was over the movie was continued, but after fifteen minutes General Quarters was sounded again. After this second raid the movie was continued, but with the same drastic result. This procedure continued all night, but the crew was stubborn, and after a raid at 0500 the movie was complete.

In the first forty eight hours at Kerama Retto we spent eleven hours at Battle Stations, particularly at night. During the day we would watch the crippled ships painfully craw in from picket stations. They would limp in, many of them still smoking, and would drop anchor to wait until the overworked repair men gave them their attention and assistance. If the Navy never before fought gallantly, they made up for it now. It took a lot of courage to go out on that picket line, for the chances of getting badly damaged or sunk were at least one out of three. The momentous struggle going on out there was never more evident to us than at Kerama Retto where we could watch the valiant picket ships come limping in, and there were many that never did come in. On one occasion a destroyer minesweeper came in asking and pleading for an immediate berth, for she had a number of men trapped alive in a compartment in a flooded section of the ship.

BACK TO THE PICKET STATION :

We were ready for sea on May thirteenth and were ordered to proceed to Nagushi anchorage for assignment to a picket station. At noon of this very day we were assigned to a radar picket station about forty miles West of Okinawa. We proceeded at high speed and relieved one of the destroyers at that station a short time later. This station was a very active one, and we were almost sure to have some opposition. At this station were the *Smith* DM-23 , who is in our division, and the destroyer *Casson Young* DD-793

Our patrol was in the immediate vicinity of Kume Shima. Kume Sima was at that time a Jap held island and was about seven miles in length. It was known that a small air strip was on the island that had been used occasionally, but at present it was not a threat.

At 0200 on the morning of the thirty first we were called to Battle Stations, the danger was over thirty minutes later and we secured from Battle Stations and went back to bed. At 0300 we were called to Battle Stations once more. This was also a short length of time, approximately thirty five minutes. This was all the action we had that night and therefore it was quite uneventful. During the day we were summoned twice to Battle Stations, but the approaching planes on both occasions turned out to be friendly. The weather was now quite clear and a formidable number of protective aircraft were assigned to our sector. From the number of aircraft in the area and reports we received, it became quite obvious that they were expecting heavy air operations by the now desperate enemy. So, with a heavy air of expectancy hovering over us, the picket ships steamed serenely along.

MISTAKEN IDENTITY AND IT'S NEAR CONSEQUENCE :

" Dusk Alert--All hands man your Battle Stations ". These were the words that came over the speaker system at 1900 June first. These words were very routine by now, therefore each man manned his station without to much haste. All stations reported in as being manned, and the ship was ready for come what may. As the sun receded in the West our protective cover of fighter aircraft started back for the sanctuary of Yontan Airfield at Okinawa, leaving us quite alone.

There were three picket ships on this station, the destroyer *Young* DD-793, the *Smith* DM-23 and us, the *Fraser* DM-24. Also to be found were a number of small craft (LCI's) that followed us around like prospective undertakers, for there job was to pick up the survivors when and if we were hit. The three of us lined up in a column one behind the other, so as to be able to lend greater fire power to our beams in case of an air attack, and this is the formation that we held.

Our " combat Air Patrol " had not been gone very long when over the battle phones came the voice of a lookout, " Two unidentified planes flying close to the water astern ". A few other lookouts verified this report adding that the planes were a considerable distance away. " Planes are friendly TBF's (Navy torpedo bombers) came the words from control. A few sighs of relief were omitted, and all was serene. A minute or so later ; " They may be friendly, But they are flying very close to the water and are closing the distance to us ", remarked another voice. " Yes, for friendly planes they are acting very hostile ", chimed in another talker. By this time the leading plane was travelling parallel to us and was up on our starboard bow. Presently the plane turned in and was heading toward the *Smith*. " Watch it !, he has dropped a fish ", came an excited voice.

About this time we opened up with every gun that could get on the target and no one waited for permission to fire. But the element of surprise was the enemy's and immediately he turned away and fled, but his aim was poor, for his torpedo was launched at the *Smith* and she received no damage.

It was now realized that the second plane was making a run on us, so we concentrated our fire on him. He kept closing until it became to hot for him, and then he launched his torpedo blindly and turned away. Fortunately his aim was poor also, and we came through unscathed. All during this attack the ship was going through frantic maneuvers in hope of throwing the enemy off, and it was a combination of alertness, volume of gun fire and skillful handling of the ship that pulled us through that night.

For a number of days after this incident " Control " had their hands full attempting to keep the gun watches from firing at unwary friendly planes that came too close. Who could blame these men ? This was the second time that a so called friendly plane attempted to destroy us.

A DEMONSTRATION OF TEAMWORK :

We were alerted again in the morning due to an unidentified plane being in the immediate vicinity, but the plane proved itself to be friendly and all was serene. The weather which was by now quite cloudy proved to be an advantage out at this patrol station. During the day we had a combat air patrol around us and at dusk alert that night they informed us that they had sighted about thirty Japs in a small boat near an island in our patrol sector. We never bothered to investigate them and they never did prove to be a threat.

At 0200 on the morning of June third we were alerted. A total of six enemy raids came in on Okinawa, mostly from the Northeast. The night fighters that intercepted them made a very impressive showing and the Japanese pilots did not score many successes on that early morning attack. With the advent of a single enemy plane in our area at 0800 we again trudged to Battle Stations but the wily enemy kept well out of range. With the arrival of our combat air patrol was the simultaneous departure of the enemy who winged it home at a fast clip.

Our air coverage was increased to four Corsairs (generally piloted by Marine flyers) that morning and at noon they were joined by Navy Hellcats. This picket station now had twelve protective fighters and it was obvious to us all that heavy daylight air attacks were expected that afternoon. Fortunately with poor visibility and overcast skies we had the weather as an asset.

At 1300 we went to Battle Stations as enemy raids began to appear. The aircraft were coming in from the Northeast and there were a large number of aircraft in each raid. The combat air patrol had a fine opportunity to display their dexterity as they intercepted the raiders. Their experience paid dividends and a large number of Japanese airmen never knew what hit them. All picket stations received excellent support that day. An enemy fighter was shot down on our starboard quarter about two miles away. He was sighted and intercepted by approximately five Hellcats. These Navy flyers were remarkable. They all raced head on at the Jap and when they were very close they executed a complicated maneuver that sent them wheeling off in different directions and in the space of a few seconds they had boxed the Jap in and splashed him into the water. This action had been carried out so smoothly and with precision that it was hard to believe if it wasn't for the Japanese plane burning in the water.

Later the *Smith* DM-23 left us temporarily to pick up the pilot of one of our own aircraft. It seems that two of our aircraft collided in midair. There was scuttlebutt spreading about the ship to the effect that Japanese planes were using American markings

OUR SQUADRON IS SMALLER :

The Japanese made further efforts that evening, therefore at 1900 the general alarm summoned us to General Quarters. The enemy raids were concentrated on the northern part of Okinawa where the Americans were wiping up the enemy troop remnants. The night fighters scored a number of successes and four enemy " Bettys " were splashed almost simultaneously. This day would be our last at this station. It was the conclusion of five days at " Bogie Junction ".

The dreaded typhoon season was in full swing and the Okinawa area was threatened, everything loose had to be lashed down tight.

We were finally relieved from our post and we headed back to Kerama Retto at noon to receive fuel, stores, ammo and mail. On the morning of June fifth we refueled and departed for Okinawa. The storm was no longer a threat now, but the enemy was still making his presence known. While anchored in Hagushi Anchorage we went to Battle Stations twice. The enemy came in from the West in small raids and one Kamikaze succeeded in suiciding into the cruiser *Louisville* CA-28. About 1600 on June sixth enemy raids appeared to the North and Northwest ; the enemy was intercepted forty miles away, where many of them were splashed. By now the weather had cleared, and it was bright and sunny.

This same day we were ordered to proceed to a station four miles East of Okinawa where we were to screen the harbor. We were to relieve the *Ditter* DM-31, who was the screening ship there at the time. We went to " Sunset Alert " as we proceeded to our new assignment. About this time the enemy aircraft were detected as they were approaching the area. It was a beautiful and clear night, the first we had in quite a while.

The enemy were approaching in large numbers to the station which we were assigned for a concentrated attack. By the time we arrived there, the enemy had been driven off, but the *Ditter* was in pitiful condition. She was so badly damaged that she had to be towed back to Kerama Retto and eventually placed out of commission. The ship assigned to tow her back was a minelayer of our division, the *Bauer* DM-26. She was companion of the *Ditter* on this station and had also been hit. She was not as badly hit as the *Ditter* and was quite capable of towing her back. The *Bauer* was out of action almost four months, and they later found a five hundred pound bomb lodged in one of her tanks. So it was that two more minelayers would be out of action, one for a few months, and the other permanently. Slowly but surely, the Okinawa campaign was cutting the minelayers down until now only five out of the original twelve had not been damaged.

A MINE SWEEPING OPERATION :

This was a very busy station, as we had found out promptly, and within twenty four hours we had six air alerts. On the night of June eighth, eleven raids approached Okinawa from our direction, and the enemy knew our approximate location, for they were searching for us. Fortunately, it was pitch black, and in view of the fact that we were completely darkened, it was next to impossible to locate us. On one occasion, an enemy plane came within seven hundred yards of our fantail without detecting us. Though we did a great deal of anti-aircraft firing at this station, there were times it proved wisest to keep silent. On June ninth we were relieved and returned to Okinawa.

There was scuttlebutt that another operation was coming off shortly, and that we would participate in it. However, everything remained quiet at Kerama Retto and we enjoyed a little rest. It was later we were informed that the destroyer *Porter* was sunk, and that all hands on board were rescued. Finally the official word came through confirming the scuttlebutt ; we would participate in the coming mine sweeping operation.

On June twelfth the *Wiley* DM-29 and we got under way for a preliminary investigation of the area of the operation. It was only about a six hour round trip, for the area was just South of Okinawa. The Captain, however was taking every precaution necessary. We went to General Quarters right after we got underway and did not secure until three hours later, when we started back to base. Since the operation was carried out at 0100 , we lost some sleep, but we were well rested. We returned to Kerama Retto and refueled, that night we departed with the minesweepers. There were only five minelayers capable of assisting in this operation, all the others had been badly damaged by enemy aircraft while serving on the Okinawa picket line, and were out of the combat area.

The operation commenced the next morning, and it was quite novel to us the first day. Most of us stayed topside and all compartments were sealed so that if we hit a mine, we would be prepared for it. But after the first day we no longer bothered to stay topside, and carried out our routine work with the nonchalance that would be displayed if we were tied to a dock.

It was not until the fourth day of the operation that any mines were brought to the surface. We destroyed three of the mines that were brought to the surface.

They were just as powerful and destructive as imagination leads us to believe. It was necessary to take shelter from flying shrapnel that was originally the housing of the explosive. Even though the mine was from one half to one mile away, it was still a dangerous device to destroy.

While we were sweeping this area, the Japs were subjecting Okinawa to heavy attacks. The destroyer *Twiggs* DD-591, on picket duty, was sunk and one hundred eighty men were rescued. Only on one occasion did enemy aircraft approach us, and this was a single plane that came within fifteen miles.

THE OKINAWA CAMPAIGN IS OVER :

This was a brazen enemy, he closed to within twelve miles of us before Navy Wildcats sent him home, racing at a high altitude. It was quite apparent that the enemy command was curious as to what we were doing, but he was never able to have his planes approach closer than twelve miles. Though he had a good idea as to what we were doing, he did not know how we were progressing.

We returned to Kerama Retto on the twentieth of June to fuel and receive mail, for one phase of our operation had been completed. On the following day, about 1800 we heard the twenty millimeter guns open up near at hand, and the heavier barking of the large caliber guns mingled with the chatter of the twenties. The general alarm sounded, but we were already on our way to Battle Stations, and the frantic anti-aircraft fire spurred us to greater speed. It instantly brought to my mind the surprise attack on the *New Mexico* a short while back. As it turned out both instances were surprisingly similar.

It seems that an enemy plane approached our sanctuary undetected and circled the anchored units with deliberate care. When he located his target he came in at low speed, and it was then that he was recognized as enemy. All guns that could bear on him did so, he had dropped a bomb on the USS *Curtiss* AV-4, which was a large conspicuous seaplane tender. As he banked away from the stricken ship, anti-aircraft fire pounced upon him with great accuracy, and he turned, after being hit, in an attempt to suicide into the damaged tender. However, he fell short and exploded in the water in what might be technically called a near miss on the tender.

It appears that the senior officer in command of Kerama Retto had his quarters on board the tender, and the Japanese were out to get him. They sent two Kamikaze pilots out to knock out the seaplane tenders, (as the scuttlebutt goes). Each pilot carried a crude map with an " X " marking the approximately position of the tenders. This is the reason that the plane was so deliberate in choosing the target. This was also scuttlebutt, but there is a good chance that it was true.

The operational commander was not hurt at all, but no more chances were taken with unidentified aircraft. This, I imagine, is the reason that we had eleven air alerts within the next twenty four hours. There were twenty raids on the following morning and they were heavy attacks. The brunt of the attack was at Okinawa, where the destroyer transport *Barry* APD-29 was sunk, and a destroyer escort had been hit during the night.

We were also informed that all organized resistance had ceased, and that bitterly contested Okinawa was won. Fleet Admiral Nimitz gave a " well done " to all men engaged in the Okinawa campaign. We knew that the fighting was not over and that air attacks would continue.

ANOTHER MINESWEEPING OPERATION :

We returned to the mine sweeping area and assisted the mine force in destroying the deadly instruments. On the twenty fourth of June we headed back to Kerama Retto, for our job was finished . While at Kerama Retto, we received tender availability and tied up alongside the destroyer tender *Hamul* AD-20. It was the *Humul* that served us as a destroyer tender at Bermuda during our shakedown.

After our availability was up, we picked up a large number of buoys from the *Weehawken* and on 4 July we got underway for another sweeping operation Northwest of Okinawa. On 5 July we had a rendezvous with the mine sweepers and the sweeping commenced. A large number of mines were detected, cut up to the surface, and destroyed by enthusiastic fire. Twice, before the operation was half completed, we returned to Okinawa for fuel, provisions and mail.

On a few occasions, enemy aircraft was sighted, but they did not venture close. It is quite obvious that he detected us, for he dropped tinfoil to foul up our bearing on him. On another occasion an enemy plane came in quite close to us, but was shot down when he reached Okinawa. On the fifteenth of July we returned to Okinawa for three days. The whole minesweeping unit was in, and most of them had been out for fifteen days.

It was quite rough the morning that we came in, and we noticed two amphibious ships being pounded to pieces where they had piled up on the reefs. There were a large number of heavy units of the fleet at Okinawa, being coincident with recent reports of the fleet bombarding Tokyo. The super cruisers *Alaska* CB-1 and *Guam* CB-2 were observed in the vicinity.

We had detected a flooded compartment below the water line and it was found that we go into drydock. We entered the drydock about 0900 and left at 1600 with effected repairs. The damage was negligible and took but half hour to repair. During the eight hours in drydock all hands on board turned to and the ship was painted and scraped and the engineering spaces cared for in that length of time. By that time everyone was weary, and then our ammunition was brought aboard. The men never worked harder or complained less since the ship went into commission.

A typhoon was expected and all ships were ordered out to sea to ride it out and so once again we were underway. The storm never did get to near us, and when all was fair we returned to Okinawa. The date was now July twenty first.

ADVENT OF THE ATOMIC BOMB :

While we were at Okinawa we picked up Comdr. Atkins, who was to replace our Captain. To lose our old Captain would be very beneficial on the morale of the crew, for he was disliked, and rightfully so. It was bad enough for all of us to have to fight the Japanese without having to fight amongst ourselves, and yet due to our old Captain's influence there was a great deal of unrest and dissatisfaction attached to every and any insignificant thing. The Captain was transferred on the twenty sixth of July and the ship was left into wiser and more competent hands.

On the twenty ninth of the month our operations were completed and we were once again at Okinawa. During the first evening at this, by now familiar place, we had two air alerts and one of our destroyers was sunk by Kamikaze pilots. We received mail back from the " States " and were able to obtain an account on the picket line for a period of two and three quarters months of operations. The picket ships went into Battle Stations one hundred and fifty times, or twice a day. These alerts sometimes lasted many hours. There were nine picket ships sunk and twenty one damaged. One fourth of the 4,907 casualties which the Navy had suffered were on picket ships. The picket ships knocked down 490 Jap planes and knocked out uncounted suicide boats. At least one out of every three picket ships were sunk or damaged.

We were scheduled to go on another operation, but it was temporarily postponed due to a threatening typhoon. On August sixth we heard the spectacular use of the Atomic bomb on the radio, and we followed the item with interest. When we were informed on August ninth that Russia declared war on Japan, we began to wonder how the Japanese people were taking it. Many of the men began to speculate on how many more weeks the war would last, and in general the spirits of the men soared to new heights.

On August tenth we departed for our mining assignment with a number of destroyer mine sweepers and the *Gwin* DM-33 . On the following day we were ordered back to Okinawa where we stood by for special assignment. We all knew that it was something special and were looking forward to it. We figured that it tied in with attempted peace proposals by the Japanese. Many of us ventured to guess that we would sweep out Tokyo Bay, but then again none of us really knew.

Early on the morning of August thirteenth a Japanese plane sneaked and managed to hit the battleship *Pennsylvania* BB-38, doing considerable damage. She needed assistance during the early hours of the morning, so she must have been damaged quite seriously.

JAPAN SURRENDERS :

It was the thirteenth of August, the morning after the attack on the *Pennsylvania*, that we received orders to get underway. As we pulled out of the bay we observed the hapless Penn listing quite badly and two vessels, one to either side of her standing close by to render her assistance. There were eight destroyer minesweepers and two destroyer minelayers in this unit of ours, the other minelayer was the *Gwin*. As it turned out, our destination was rendezvous with the Third Fleet, which was operating about three hundred miles off Tokyo. Being a fast stepping outfit, we covered the distance in a short span of time.

On August fifteenth we received the wonderful news, " The Japanese had surrendered and the war is over ! " At the time that we received this news we were one hundred and fifty miles off the Honshu coast, which is the main island of the Japanese Empire, we were just two hundred miles from Tokyo. Even though the Japanese had surrendered, the war continued until definite peace terms were signed. Many curious American airmen returning from raids on the Japanese homeland came in and gave us the once over. In vain, we asked a few of the carrier planes the location of the logistic force, but they always gave us a negative answer. It seems that they knew only the location of their own unit. So, we had quite a bit of difficulty in locating the illusive supply unit of the much more illusive task force thirty eight, but after a day of fruitless searching, we found them.

We refueled from this group, and then were temporarily assigned as screening units to their already tremendous anti-submarine screen, this whole force was tremendous in size and was capable of keeping the entire third fleet at sea for a number of months. The following day the *Gwin* and we were detached from this unit and sent to Iwo Jima to pick up mail for the third fleet. It was a welcome task, for it took us away from the monotonous screening duty for a while and enabled us to get a glimpse of Iwo Jima which had still been in a turmoil when we had left there back in the middle of March.

Then we sighted a surfaced submarine and closed the distance to him immediately. All hands were summoned to General Quarters and we were determined that this sub would not get away. As it turned out, the submarine was American, and he informed us that he was returning, to that far off Utopia known as the United States. Later we sighted another surfaced submarine which also turned out to be American and was also " Stateside Bound ". Apparently all of our subs were returning to their bases, for there was little more they could do.

A RETURN TO IWO :

We arrived at Iwo Jima on the evening of August eighteenth, and a reception committee of Army Mustangs intercepted us. A few of them that were in a playful mood made us the object of their attention. They were very fast and very maneuverable planes, we had all we could do to follow their movements. We all thought how terrible it would have been if the Japanese had a comparable plane to use for Kamikaze purposes. There is no doubt but they would have inflicted a great deal of damage.

We had all heard the story about the Japanese officer that finally came out of a cave and gave himself up to the American authorities on Iwo, and when he looked about the island he said " It's a miracle. " We were now almost close enough to witness this miracle.

For the short amount of time this Japanese officer had been hiding a few thousand Seabees had been constructing, and the amount of changes made was incredible. Mount Suribachi, old " Hot Rocks ", had it's face lifted and so much of it had been cleaned away that it was nowhere near its original magnitude.

As we got closer to the island we could see the efficiency of the industrial might of our country combined with the Seabees spirit. There were a colossal number of buildings and hangers where before there had been nothing standing at all. The island had been built into a tremendous Army base and airfield in less than six months. There is little doubt that the airfield was capable of holding well over five hundred planes. The air traffic was exceptionally heavy, there was always thirty to fifty fighters in the air, and planes were landing and taking off continuously.

Iwo Jima was a large base post office for the Navy, and where all mail from and to the third fleet was delivered. We refueled from one of those ever present naval tankers, and then we picked a large amount of mail and American and British officers that were reporting to the fleet for duty. The British officers were assigned to the British Naval units operation with the third fleet. So, with the ship loaded down we started back to the third fleet alone. The *Gwin* remained behind to pick up some mail that was expected the next day.

THE FIGHTING THIRD FLEET :

We met up with the third fleet and reported directly to Admiral Halsey's flagship, the battleship *Missouri* BB-63. This fleet was tremendous, for there were major warships all around us and extending out as far as the eye could see. We had very little difficulty locating the *Missouri*, for her revolutionary design and momentous bulk made her very conspicuous. We informed the flagship that we had mail for units of the third fleet and stood by for further orders.

We were dispatched to a particular station where we were to pass mail to the destroyers of various task forces. This fleet was so large that it was necessary to have a destroyer pick up all the mail for the unit he was attached to, other than that, we would have been passing mail for well over a week. We also transfered all our passengers in this fashion It was very amusing to watch them transfer the men, for many of them came perilously close to the water as they were pulled across the span between us and the destroyer as we travelled at fifteen knots.

The fleet was a spectacular affair and was so large that it was formed into individual units so that confusion would be at a minimum. There were always a dozen or more destroyers darting in and out through the complicated formations on a mission for their respective units. Aircraft carriers wee constantly falling in and out of formation to receive or send their flights into the air. There were always ships arriving for duty while others were leaving on scouting trips and sorties. In addition to this, ships were constantly falling in and out of formation for fuel and provisions. But the Navy efficiency was conspicuous, for it was orderly confusion

We were assigned to the unit that would spearhead the occupational forces and the flagship was the mighty battleship *Iowa* BB-61. The unit or task force was composed of destroyer minesweepers, the *Gwin* DM-33 and us, and the anti-aircraft cruiser *San Diego* CL-53, a few escorts and a small number of transports and provision ships. On one occasion we had an opportunity to refuel from the *Iowa* and found her to be a very fine ship. I never saw so many guns on a single ship before, and the ship was as neat as a pin.

We were to be the first units to enter Tokyo Bay and were just waiting for the order to start in. With the war actually over, every hour of waiting seemed like a month and the crew was getting restless. A few fanatical Japanese airmen had made sporadic suicide attacks on the third fleet without success. Admiral Halsey informed the fleet that the Japanese were no longer an enemy, and that when we saw a Jap plane to shoot him down in a friendly fashion.

WE ENTER SAGAMI WAN :

We were soon joined by the backbone of the minecraft in the Pacific, the group of light minesweepers. These small vessels proceeded every invasion that was conducted, they were rugged little ships manned by tough crews, with perhaps the most dangerous duty to minesweeping preceding invasions. It was the twenty eighth of August that we were to enter Tokyo Bay, and we would have been in commission just one year and six days. In the course of this time we have traveled 55,000 miles and burned 3,000,000 gallons of fuel. We have made and consumed 3,250,000 gallons of fresh water and have been summoned to Battle Stations one hundred and twenty three times. The longest sustained air attack kept us at our Battle Stations for ten consecutive hours. The longest actual General Quarters we had was at Iwo Jima, where we remained at our Battle Stations for eighteen consecutive hours.

Now here we were , approaching the shores of Japan, and though we were well over thirty miles from the shore of our enemy, we can already make out land. This is because of Mt. Fujiyama, the famous volcano and landmark of Japan, which rises thousands of feet above the mountainous terrain of the eastern coast of Honshu. All hands went to Battle Stations before we were to anchor in the bay in Sagami Wan, it would be foolish to trust such a treacherous country as Japan.

We were not the first arrivals at Sagami Wan. On the contrary, there were a very large number of all types of naval craft in there before us, but that was because there was no longer danger of mines. The heavy units of the fleet were the first in, and they anchored close to the beach where they could train their guns on targets that might attempt to oppose the anchoring of the allied naval forces. All these heavy units were strategically placed so that they formed a ring of protective steel around the main forces at the anchorage.

In no time at all the small whaleboats were observed scurrying from one vessel to another, and this always symbolized to me that the Navy had the situation well in hand. All men were supposed to remain at Battle Stations until further notice and though we had been at General Quarters since 1500 , no word came through to secure during the long night. It was quite obvious that if the Japanese were to attempt anything we were prepared for it. Never again would the Japanese be taken as trustworthy.

WE ENTER TOKYO BAY :

Here was the big day, the day we were to enter Tokyo Bay. We were the third ship to go in. Directly ahead of us were two destroyer minesweepers and bringing up the rear was the *San Diego* CL-53 and her escorts plus a seaplane tender and a temporary communications ship. As we started through the narrow entrance we were all keyed up to a high point in jubilation, but not once were we anything but intensely alert. We knew that the Japs would not welcome us, for the vanquished were a very proud people with fanatical spirit.

The large coastal defense guns cleverly camouflaged and aligned along the entrance on both sides had white flags across their deadly muzzles. From the number of them and their positions it appeared that nothing would be able to enter the bay if they decided against it, and I was certainly glad they were for once abiding by their word. Overhead we had a large number of fighter aircraft to ward off any enemy planes that might want to expend themselves as some Jap airmen had done without the sanction of their government We could observe some large modern buildings that were Red Cross establishments. They had a very large flag with a red cross on it, and the tops of the buildings were painted with large red crosses. At this time my mind drifted back to the episode of the hospital ship, the USS *Comfort* AH-6.

There was little else of interest as we continued through the mouth of the bay, for everything seemed dead somewhat as if the Japanese civilians had dug in as did the Japanese soldiers on Iwo Jima.

We anchored close to the Yokosuka Naval Base and here as everything else, work had stopped. There was a few sunken vessels in the shallow water that had been the targets of carrier aircraft in raids of the past. We noticed a Jap destroyer that had run up on some reefs and was slowly being pounded to shreds. A distance from the Yokosuka Naval Base was the battleship *Nagota*, which was beached and badly damaged by carrier aircraft strikes. All in all it was the appearance of a defeated country.

The communication ship was sending out on the spot accounts of this small unit that proceeded the fleet into Tokyo Bay. In this broadcast they listed the *San Diego* as being the first ship in, whereas in reality she was the fourth. At a later broadcast they listed every one of the units that entered the bay except us, the crew was quite mad, for up to this date we had no recognition for any of the work we had done. Our Captain signaled this communication ship by light and gave them the details. They apologized for having neglected to mention us and promised to do so in their next broadcast. It is very doubtful that they made another broadcast.

THE PEACE TERMS ARE SIGNED :

On Sunday 2 September 1945, the peace terms were signed on board the USS *Missouri* BB-63. The *Missouri*, as well as the rest of the fleet, entered Tokyo Bay on 29 August 1945, and the third fleet really filled the anchorage. The British units came in on the following day and this completed the setting. The *Iowa* BB-61 and the *Missouri* BB-63, two of the most powerful battleships afloat, were riding at anchor side by side. In addition to this the British battleships *Duke of York* and *King George* were anchored near by. In addition to this, the numerous powerful cruisers and more numerous large destroyers of the third fleet were everywhere to be seen. It was an impressive display of Allied might.

Two Japanese submarines passed us close by with American crews aboard and the Japanese sailors lined up on the deck. There is one notable thing about Japanese submarines and that is their size, they are tremendous or tiny. To offset this picture, fifteen or more trim American submarines of an identical design arrived in colorful regalia and anchored near at hand. It was gratifying to see these undersea craft participate in the unconditional surrender of Japan.

In the background of the Allied might was the symbol of the vengeance that Allied might can lash out--the gutted and blackened city of Yokohama, and the burned and beached battleship being the most conspicuous.

The peace terms were signed on an overcast day, but regardless there were hundred of American planes that put on a very impressive show. The vaunted Super fortresses appeared in terrifying numbers and the sky was literally blackened about with various types of aircraft. Today the war was in every significance of the word " over ". This ship of a non-combatant class was able to enter Tokyo Bay with the preliminary forces and had managed to survive and give a good account of itself in the Okinawa picket line. But in view of the fact that a minelayer is certainly not exposed to danger and actually sees no action, they should be engaged in post-war work out here. The combat vessels should be the ones to return home to participate in victory celebrations. After all, it is necessary to be fair, and they were exposed to danger. We men aboard the USS *Thomas E. Fraser* DM-24 heartily agree with this view point. But our job is actually beginning for there are a great deal of enemy mines through this whole area from Formosa to Northern Japan which are to be cleared away. So now, at this present moment we are doing this job and shall continue to destroy these vicious devices, the deadly mines, until there is not a mine left in the Pacific.

****

In September, the minelayer operated with sweep units clearing mines in Kii Suido, in Wakayama anchorage, and off the Pacific coast of the Japanese islands. While anchored in Wakanoura Wan on the 17th and 18th, she weathered a typhoon whose 100-knot gusts forced her to use her engines to ease the strain on her anchor. When the storm abated, she sent out a party to aid survivors and to remove confidential gear and publications from YMS-478 which had broached and capsized.

She continued off the Japanese coast into October. Following a week at Buckner Bay, she got underway on 25 October for a new sweep area in the East China Sea. Assigned to lay buoys and to assist in navigation the warship operated in the northern reaches of the East China Sea into November. On 17 November, she put in at Sasebo for fuel and upkeep. On 1 December, she broke out her homeward bound pennant, and the next day departed Japan, steaming via Eniwetok and Pearl Harbor, and arriving in San Diego on 22 December.

On the 26th, she got underway and steamed via the Canal Zone to Norfolk, arriving there on 8 January 1946. Late in March, the destroyer minelayer put in at Charleston for overhaul and remained in that port until late in the year when she participated in a reserve training cruise with *Wisconsin* (BB-64) which continued into January 1947. From February until May, she operated out of various Caribbean ports; then returned to Norfolk. On the last day of June, she departed Hampton Roads with *Shannon* (DM-25) and *Palau* (CVE-122) and steamed to Recife, Brazil ; then proceeded on to the African port of Monrovia, Liberia for a courtesy and good-will visit during

Liberia's centennial celebration. After stopping at Dakar, French West Africa, she returned to the east coast on 16 August.

The destroyer minelayer continued operations off the Atlantic coast ranging as far north as Argentia, Newfoundland and as far south as the Caribbean. As the emissary of the United States Government, the USS *Thomas E. Fraser* (DM-24) was ordered by the U.S. Navy to the shores of the Hudson River at Tarrytown, New York to participate with the townspeople in observing the Nations first " Veterans Day ". This is a National Holiday observed on November 11th. (Armistice Day), the anniversary of the armistice of World War I. Veterans Day is now observed by the nation to honor her heros whose lives were taken in the conflict of both World Wars I and II and to the service personnel who returned home to their familys. The citizens of Tarrytown were welcomed aboard the *Fraser* to see how a man of war operated and how her crew lives.

On 1 December 1947, she was immobilized; but she was again back in service by May 1949. Following local operations out of Guantanamo in July, the ship departed Hampton Roads early in August and called at Cherbourg, France, before returning to the caribbean where she remained until she returned to Charleston in November.

In September 1950, she broke the routine of training operations off the east coast with a Mediterranean deployment which continued until 22 January 1951 when she departed Oran. In June , she was again underway for European ports, this time on a midshipman cruise which took her to Copenhagen, Plymouth, and Lisbon. In July , she visited Cuba before returning to the east coast. For the next three years, she varied exercises off the Atlantic coast and in the Caribbean with brief voyages to Europe.

In February 1955, she engaged in mine planting off Key West in support of a fleet service mine test program, one of her last assignments. On 10 June 1955 she was placed in reserve ; and , on 12 September, she was decommissioned and placed in reserve at Portsmouth, NH Naval Shipyard. Her name was struck from the Navy list on 1 November 1970.

Thomas E. Fraser (DM-24) received three battle stars for World War II service.

WHERE THE FLEET GOES, WE'VE BEEN !

WELL DONE TO ALL

WELL DONE

courtsey of Milton Hackett

Nevett Brooke Atkins

United States Naval Academy   Class of 1935

"Tommy"   "Usnar"   "Marty"

At Large

HAIL the martyr, folks; the man with the proper attitude.

He always keeps himself one thirty inch step ahead of the men with the swords. Brooke is Navy-born, the sea is in his blood, and as long as there's wind in his sails, he hopes to keep up the family tradition. They like it , those Atkins boys. Usnar lives by the books, smokes Chesterfields, tells a mean story if you give him time, and handles any situation with a manner that only three years in Brazil can give. Tommy has shown that he can take it by doing a four year stretch with the suicide club; but, he trained by dinning out at every opportunity.

courtsey of the "Lucky Bag", United States Naval Academy

Robert H. Smith

United States Naval Academy   Class of 1920

Robert Holmes Smith, born in Harrellsville, N.C., 8 August 1898, graduated from the U.S. Naval Academy 6 June 1919. After duty in various surface ships, he served with the Submarine Service for 17 years. He commanded *Bonita*, was an instructor at the New London submarine school, a member of the Naval Academy staff, Submarine Gunnery Officer with the Bureau of Navigation, Navigation Officer in *Pennsylvania,* and Chief of Staff for Submarine Division, Atlantic Patrol Force. Following promotion to Captain, he commanded *Sperry* in the Pacific from May 1942 to January 1943, and was Commander of Squadron 2, Pacific Submarine Fleet, when he died in an airplane crash in California 21 January 1943.

National Archives

USS ROBERT H. SMITH (DD735) (DM-23)

(DM-23 ; dp. 2,200 ; l. 376' 6" ; b. 40' 10" ; dr. 18' 10" ; s. 34k.; cpl. 363 ; a. 6 5", 12 40mm., 8 20mm., 2 dct., 4 dep. ; cl. *Robert H. Smith*)

USS *Robert H. Smith* was laid down as hull # 735 0n 10 January 1944 at the Bath Iron Works, Bath Maine; launched 25 May 1944; sponsored by Mrs. Robert Holmes Smith; redesignated as (DM-23) a destroyer minelayer on 19 July 1944, and commissioned on 4 August 1944, Commander Henry Farrow in command.

After training off Bermuda, *Smith* transited the Panama Canal with a Pacific bound convoy on 28 November 1944, to enter the Pacific War; *Smith* arrived at Pearl Harbor on 21 December to begin her duties. On 27 January *Smith* escorted a convoy of the 5th Amphibious Corps bound for Iwo Jima. During final amphibious rehersals off Saipan, *Smith* rescued the crew of a downed B-29. She arrived off Iwo Jima early in the morning on the 19 February 1945 just in time for the landings. For most of the next three weeks *Smith* served as a radar picket ship fifty miles north of Iwo Jima controlling CAP and reporting radar contacts. *Smith* also bombarded shore positions on Iwo Jima and acted as a screening vessel for night retirement formations.

Smith departed Iwo Jima 9 March, escorted a group of merchantmen as far as Saipan; and then sailed for Ulithi, arriving there 13 March. On 25 March, *Smith* arrived at Kerama Retto with a group of minesweepers to make a check sweep at Kerama Retto and the invasion beaches of Okinawa. During the pre-assault period, *Smith* was twice attack by kamikaze planes but fended them off without any casualties. *Smith* also acted as support ship for the minesweepers, and stood picket line duty and acted as a screening escort for night time withdrawals. During the landings *Smith* screened the transport area and then departed on 5 April 1945 with a convoy for Guam. On her return 21 April, *Smith* undertook six weeks of radar picket duty, underwent numerous kamikaze attacks and splashed five enemy planes. On 4 June 1945 , *Smith* completed her tour of duty as a picket line ship. She spent a few more days screening the Okinawa transport area and supporting the amphibious attack on Iheya Shima.

Smith left on 13 June to begin the long tedious task as a support vessel for clearing the naval mines that had been laid by Japanese forces in the East China Sea area near Miyako Shima in the southern Ryukyus. They were protected by planes from an escort carrier group and *Smith* acted as primary fighter director ship. The operation lasted until 25 June and the next order of business was to sweep the central area of the East China Sea about 100 miles east of Shanghai; in this operation *Smith* acted as a radar buoy layer and small craft supply ship in addition to her duties as fighter director ship. In July, *Smith* departed Okinawa for a large mine field in the northern portion of the East China Sea about 100 miles southwest of Kyushu, the southern most island of the main Japanese islands. They had barely started sweeping it when word came of the surrender of Japan. *Smith* and other ships, were suddenly ordered to sweep a channel through the Yellow Sea for the occupation ports of Korea for the 7th Amphibious Corps and *Smith* led a convoy of transport ships through that channel on 7 September 1945. *Smith* then proceeded to Sasebo to help with cutting a channel through the mine field into that port. After working in the Sasebo area for some time, *Smith* was forced to ride out several typhoons in the Sea of Japan. *Smith* then joined a group of larger minesweepers to sweep Van Diemen Straits south of the island of Kyushu. *Smith* then operated in the Yellow Sea with a large group of minesweepers, and made a courier run from Sasebo to Kiirun to support minesweepers working in the straits of Formosa, returning to Sasebo by way of Shanghai.

On 17 January 1946 *Smith* sailed for the United States, reaching San Francisco 7 February 1946. On 29 January 1947, *Smith* was placed out of commission in reserve and attached to the San Diego Group, Pacific Reserve Fleet. *Smith* was reclassified MMD-23 on 1 January 1969. She remained a part of the Pacific Reserve Fleet until 1971, when after being surveyed, *Smith* was found unfit for further duty and was stricken from the Navy List on 26 February 1971. Her ultimate fate , *Robert H. Smith* (DM-23) was sold for scrap metal.

Robert H. Smith (DM-23) earned five battle stars for World War II service.

Thomas E. Fraser

United States Naval Academy   Class of 1924

Thomas Edward Fraser - born on 6 February 1901 in Stafford Springs, Connecticut - was appointed to the United States Naval Academy on 3 September 1920. After graduating on 4 June 1924, he served in *Wyoming* (BB-32) for nearly a year and studied torpedo warfare at the Naval Torpedo Station, Newport, R.I., before reporting for duty on board *Worden* (DD-288) on 17 January 1926. He served in that destroyer until 1 May 1930. Following assignments in *Ellis* (DD-154) and at the New York Navy Yard, Fraser reported on 1 March 1934 for duties in connection with the fitting out of *Tuscaloosa* (CA-37). Assignments to the Philadelphia and Portsmouth Navy Yards followed in the late 1930's.

During 1940 and 1941, he briefly commanded, in turn, destroyers *Yarnall* (DD-143), *Claxton* (DD-140), and *Broome* (DD-210). On 10 November 1941, he became commanding officer of *Walke* (DD-416) and, on 20 August 1942, he was appointed to the temporary rank of Commander.

National Archives

USS THOMAS E. FRASER (DM-24)

(DM-24 : dp. 2,200 ; I. 376' 6" ; b. 40' 10" ; dr. 18' 10" ; s.34.2k.; cpl. 363 ; a. 6 5", 12 40mm.,
8 20mm., ; 2 .50-cal. mg. ; cl. *Robert H. Smith*)

Thomas E. Fraser (DM-24) was laid down as DD-736 on 31 January 1944 at Bath, Maine, by
the Bath Iron Works ; named *Thomas E. Fraser* on 1 March 1944 ; launched on 10 June 1944 ;
sponsored by Mrs. Thomas E. Fraser ; reclassified as a destroyer minelayer and redesignated
DM-24 on 20 July 1944 ; and commissioned on 22 August 1944 , Comdr. Ronald Joseph
Woodaman in command.

National Archives

Colonel Harold D. Shannon

Harold D. Shannon, born on 16 September 1892 at Chicago, Ill., enlisted in the United States Marine Corps on 17 October 1913 and served in Mexico in 1914. On 5 July 1917, he was appointed Second Lieutenant in the Marine Corps Reserve and was subsequently commissioned Second Lieutenant in the Marine Corps. From October 1917 through the end of World War I, he served in France and was awarded the Silver Star and the Croix de Guerre for his actions during the Belleau Wood Campaign. In October 1919, he returned to the United States.

Over the next 20 years, he served at various stations in the United States and completed tours in Santo Domingo, Nicaragua, and the Panama Canal Zone. In July 1941, he was transferred from San Diego to Pearl Harbor; and, in September 1941, to Midway Island. He was awarded the Distinguished Service Medal for his leadership in the defense of that island during the Battle of Midway.

Col. Shannon remained on Midway into August. He was then transferred to Pearl Harbor; and, in October, to San Diego where he died on 16 February 1943.

The second Shannon DM-25 was named for Col. Harold D. Shannon.

National Archives

USS SHANNON (DM-25)

(DM-25 ; dp. 2,200 ; l. 376' 6" ; b. 40' 10" ; dr. 18' 10" ; s. 34k. ; cpl. 363 ; a. 6 5", 12 40mm., 8 20mm., 2 dct., 4 dcp. ; cl. *Robert H. Smith*)

Shannon (DD-737) was laid down on 14 February 1944 by the Bath Iron Works, Bath, Maine ; launched on 24 June 1944 ; sponsored by Mrs. Harold D. Shannon ; reclassified DM-25 on 19 July 1944 : and commissioned on 8 September 1944, Comdr. E.L. Foster in command.

Completing shakedown in the Bermuda area in late October, *Shannon* was ordered to overtake convoy GUS-54 and deliver election ballots before proceeding to Norfolk for availability. She accomplished her mission; completed the yard work; and on 21 November, *Shannon* departed San Diego in company with USS *Thomas E. Fraser* (DM-24) and USS *Harry F. Bauer* (DM-26) and steamed for the Pacific. On the 25th. *Shannon* rescued two crewmen from a scout plane from the *Tuscaloosa* (CA-37). On 27 January, 1945, as flagship of Mindiv 7 and a unit of force 51; *Shannon* departed Pearl Harbor for Eniwetok, Saipan, and Iwo Jima. At the latter island, on 19 February, she conducted antisubmarine patrols as the marines landed; then, during the afternoon, she moved in to provide fire support. For the next five days, she rotated between those duties; then returned to Saipan to escort reinforcements and resupply echelons to the embattled island.

She returned to Iwo Jima on 3 March and resumed duty- night illumination, harassing fire, and call fire- in support of the 4th Marine Division for another five days. On the 8th, she sailed for Ulithi; and on the 19th, she left the Western Carolines for the Ryukyus and operation " Iceberg," the invasion of Okinawa.

Shannon arrived off Kerama Retto, an island group west of Okinawa, on 25 March and covered minesweeping units and underwater demolition teams until that base was secured. She then protected the minesweepers as they prepared the way for the landings on Okinawa. On 1 April, when the troops were landed on the Hagushi beaches, she patrolled to the east of Kerama Retto; then moved to the southern coast of Okinawa to screen the demonstration landings there. Further screening duties followed; and on the 4th, she retired to the rear area. On the 15th, she returned to Okinawa and resumed screening duties. On the 21st, she commenced anti-small-boat patrols off southeastern Okinawa. She alternated that duty with radar picket duty until mid-June with interruptions only to cover minesweepers in the Tori Shima area on 11 May and in the Iheya Shima area from 30 May to 3 June.

From mid-June through the end of July, *Shannon* accompanied minesweeping units as they continued sweeping operations in the immediate Okinawa area and in the East China Sea. During the first part of August, she was at Buckner Bay for availability. On the 12th, she resumed operations with the minesweepers which continued until the war ended on the 15th.

After the cessation of hostilities in the Pacific, *Shannon* moved into the Yellow Sea with the mine units to clear the fields off Korea. On 7 September, she got underway for Japan; and , into November, she assisted the minesweeping detachments as they cleared the sea lanes to the major ports of that country. Then, having relinquished flagship duties in October, she headed back for the United States. After stops in Hawaii and on the west coast, she continued on to the east coast to join the Atlantic Fleet.

Arriving in the Chesapeake Bay in April 1946, she conducted limited operations under ComDesLant and ComSubLant into June. She then proceeded to Charleston for duty in MinDiv 2. During 1947, her operations were extended; and, that summer on the last day of June, with the *Thomas E. Fraser* DM-24 , she escorted *Palau* (CVE-122) on a goodwill visit to Recife, Brazil ; then proceeded on to the African port of Monrovia, Liberia for a courtesy and good-will visit during Liberia's centennial celebration. After stopping at Dakar, French West Africa she returned to the East coast on 16 August. Availability and limited operations followed that cruise; then , from November 1947 into August 1948, she remained immobilized at Charleston. In August 1948, she resumed operations with Mine Force, Atlantic Fleet which she continued for the next seven years. During that time, she participated in various exercises- type, fleet, and international; conducted midshipmen cruises; and deployed to the Mediterranean once, from September 1950 to January 1951. Ordered inactivated in 1955, she joined the Charleston Group, Atlantic Reserve Fleet, on 7 July and was decommissioned on 24 October. Reclassified MMD-25 on 14 August 1968, she remained in the reserve fleet until struck from the Navy list on 1 November 1970. She was subsequently sold for scrapping to the Boston Metals Co., Baltimore, MD., and was delivered to that firm in May 1973.

Shannon earned four battle stars during World War II.

Harry F. Bauer

United States Naval Academy   Class of 1927

Harry Frederick Bauer was born 17 July 1904 at Camp Thomas Lytle, Ga., and graduated from the Naval Academy in 1927. During the early part of his career he served at shore stations, including a tour as instructor at the Naval Academy, and in *Twiggs, Cuyama,* and *Tracy.* Bauer was commissioned Lieutenant Commander 1 July 1941 and took command of fast transport *Gregory* (APD-3) 1 January 1942. While acting as combat transports for Marines off Guadalcanal during the night of 4-5 September 1942, *Gregory* (APD-3) and *Little* (APD-4) were surprised by three Japanese destroyers covering a small troop landing. Though vastly outgunned, the two transports fought valiantly before being sunk. Lt. Comdr. Bauer was badly wounded, and while being pulled clear by two of his crew ordered them to rescue another man crying out for assistance. Lt. Comdr. Bauer was lost, receiving the Silver Star posthumously for his gallantry.

National Archives

USS HARRY F. BAUER (DM-26)

(DM-26 : dp. 2200 ; i. 376'6" ; b. 40'10" ; dr. 15'8" ; s. 34k. ; cpl. 336 ; a. 6 5", 8 20mm., 2 .50 cal.; cl. Robert H. Smith)

Harry F. Bauer (DM-26) was launched as DD-738 by the Bath Iron Works Corp., Bath, Maine, 9 July 1944; sponsored by Mrs. Harry F. Bauer, wife of Lt. Comdr. Bauer; reclassified (DM-26) destroyer minelayer June 1944; and commissioned 22 September 1944, Comdr. R.C. Williams, Jr. in command. Following shakedown training out of Bermuda and minelayer training off Norfolk, Harry F. Bauer sailed 28 November 1944 via the Panama Canal arriving San Diego 12 December. After additional training both there and at Pearl Harbor , Bauer departed Hawaii 27 January 1945 as a unit of Transport Group Baker for the invasion of Iwo Jima, next stop in the island campaign toward Japan. As Vice Admiral Turner's invasion troops stormed ashore 19 February, Harry F. Bauer acted as a picket vessel and carried out antisubmarine patrol to protect the transports. As the campaign developed, the ship also conducted shore bombardment, destroying several gun emplacements, tanks, and supply dumps. Bauer proceeded to Ulithi 8 March to prepare for the last and largest of the Pacific island operations, Okinawa.

Harry F. Bauer arrived Kerama Retto 25 March and helped screen minecraft during preliminary sweeps of the invasion area. Under intensive air attack during this period, Bauer shot down several Japanese planes, three on the night of 28-29 March alone. On the day of the assault, 1 April 1945, she joined the picket ships offshore, and for over two months of antisubmarine and anti-aircraft duty was under almost continuous attack. A torpedo crashed through her ballast tank 6 April, but failed to explode. At dawn, inspection revealed a torpedo was lodged just below the water line, its

61

warhead on one side of the ship and the propeller and motor on the other side. The *Bauer* was relieved later in the day and returned to Kreama Retto to have the unsightly object removed and a small patch welded over the two holes. The tail fins of the torpedo were shipped to Mrs. Harry F. Bauer, the widow of the man for whom the ship had been named. *Bauer* again shot down three aircraft on the night of 29 April 1945. While in company with *J. William Ditter* (DM-31) 6 June, she was attacked by eight enemy aircraft. Each ship accounted for three; one crashed close aboard *Bauer*, flooding two compartments. Although damaged herself, the ship escorted the crippled *J. William Ditter* (DM-31) to Kerama Retto. Survey of her damage during repairs revealed an unexploded bomb in one of her flooded compartments. *Bauer* went down to Leyte where a repair ship could deal with the unexploded bomb. When the Explosive Ordance Personnel defused the bomb, for some strange reason they laid it out on the wardroom table and someone noticed that it had stenciled on it " MADE IN BAJONNE, NEW JERSEY." Futher investigation revealed that when the defense batteries were sold that protected the entrance to Pearl Harbor in the early 1930's they were sold to the Japanese; quite naturally they took the shells for the sixteen inch guns together with the big guns themselves. Someone in the Japanese military figured out that with the addition of fins on the shells they would make fine bombs; and they did just that.

After repairs at Leyte, *Harry F. Bauer* arrived Okinawa 15 August, the day of the Japanese surrender. With the prospect of massive minesweeping in Japanese water incident to the occupation, she sailed 20 August for the East China Sea, where she engaged in minesweeping operations until arriving Sasebo 28 October. Sailing for the United States 1 December she arrived San Diego 22 December.

Sailing to Norfolk 8 January 1946, *Harry F. Bauer* began operations with the Atlantic Fleet. These consisted of antisubmarine cruises in the Atlantic and Caribbean, tactical training and fleet maneuvers. During October-November 1948 *Bauer* took part in 2nd Fleet exercises in the Atlantic, and in June-July 1949 participated in a Naval Academy training cruise with giant battleship *Missouri* (BB-63).

In 1950 *Harry F. Bauer* made her first cruise to the troubled Mediterranean, departing 9 September and returning to Charleston, SC, 1 February 1951. During the years that followed she continued with tactical operations, that took her to the Caribbean and Northern Europe. *Harry F. Bauer* ended active steaming in September 1955 and decommissioned 12 March 1956 at Charleston, entering the Atlantic Reserve Fleet, Philadelphia. Her name was struck from the Navy list on 15 August 1971 and sold for scrapping 11 June 1974.

Harry F. Bauer (DM-26) received a Presidential Unit Citation for the series of courageous actions off Okinawa during that bitter campaign, where " the fleet had come to stay " and four battle stars for World War II service.

Samuel Adams

United States Naval Academy   Class of 1935

Samuel Adams was born in Northampton, Mass., 10 April 1912. He graduated from the academy in 1935 and was designated a Naval Aviator in 1939. Lieutenant Adams, flying from *Yorktown* (CV-5), took part in the Salamaua and Lae, New Guinea raid (10 March 1942) and the battle of the Coral Sea (4-8 May 1942). He was killed 6 June 1942 during the battle of Midway.

USS ADAMS (DM-27)

(DM-27 : dp. 2,200 ; l. 376'6" ; b. 40'10" ; dr. 18'10" ; s. 34 k. ; cpl. 363 ; a. 6 5", 8 40mm., 12 20mm., 2 dct., 4 dcp., 80 mines ; cl. *Robert H. Smith*)

USS *Adams* was laid down as hull # 739 on 20 March 1944 at the Bath Iron Works, Bath, Maine. Reclassified as (DM-27), a destroyer minelayer on 19 July 1944; launched on 23 July 1944; sponsored by Mrs. Maude Ryan Adams, the widow of Lt. Samuel Adams; and commissioned at Boston, Mass., on 10 October 1944, Comdr. Henry J. Armstrong in command. After fitting out there, *Adams* embarked upon her shakedown voyage on 1 November. That cruise, which took her to Bermuda waters, lasted for the entire month. On the 29th, *Adams* headed back toward the United States and arrived at Norfolk, Va., on 3 December. Following post-shakedown availability in the navy yard there, *Adams* put to sea on 11 December with sister ship *Shea* (DM-30), bound for New York and a rendezvous with *Bennington* (CV-20). The two destroyer minelayers departed New York with the aircraft carrier on 15 December and set a course for the Panama Canal. The three warships transited the canal on 20 December and, on the 22nd, headed for the California coast. They arrived at San Diego on the 29th and remained there two days undergoing repairs. On New Years Day 1945, they got under way again, headed for Oahu, and arrived in Pearl Harbor six days latter.

For almost two months, *Adams* remained in the Hawaiian operating area. During that time, she acted as plane guard for *Bataan* (CVL-29) while the carrier conducted carrier landing qualifications for naval aviators. She also carried out gunnery exercises and shore bombardment practice. The war ship spent two periods in the Pearl Harbor Navy Yard- once for the installation of VF radar equipment and again to have her main deck plating strengthened. Early in February, *Adams* laid mines and tested mine detection equipment on them. Later the warship conducted mine laying exercises. She finished out her tour of duty in the Hawaii area late in February with another plane guard mission with *Bataan* (CVL-29).

The destroyer minelayer stood out of Pearl Harbor on 2 March, bound for the western Pacific. *Adams* arrived in Ulithi Atoll on 14 March and remained until the 19th, when she put to sea with a task group of the Okinawa invasion force. The warship saw her first combat on 23 March, the day before she arrived off Okinawa. That evening , enemy aircraft attacked her task group. *Adams* sustained her first casualties when a projectile fired from the after five-inch mount exploded prematurely killing two sailors and injuring another 13. At dawn the following day, she began minesweeping operations off Okinawa. The destroyer minelayer provided gunfire support and mine destruction services to the wooden- hulled minesweepers (AM's) doing the actual sweeping.

Those operations continued over the next few days in spite of Japanese air resistance. During that time, *Adams* was attacked by at least twelve different planes. She knocked six of her tormentors out of the air and claimed probable kills of two others. On the 28th, one of those attackers splashed about 25 feet from her port bow showering her with debris and gasoline. The damage she sustained in a collision with a salvage vessel forced her into the anchorage at Kerama Retto for emergency repairs. On 1 April, while she was operating to the southeast of Kerama Reto, a badly damaged Japanese plane splashed close aboard her stern; and what must have been two bombs exploded under her fantail causing severe damage and jamming her rudders at hard right. While *Adams* steamed in righthand circles, two more suicide planes swooped at her. *Adams* destroyed one while the other succumbed to the antiaircraft battery of *Mullany* (DD-528), the ship dispatched to assist *Adams*. Latter *Adams* was towed into Kerama Retto to begin temporary repairs alongside *Endymion* (ARL-9).

Adams departed Kerama Retto on 7 April, bound for ultimately for the United States and permanent repairs. She made stops at Guam and at Peal Harbor before arriving at the Mare Island Navy Yard on 7 May. *Adams* completed repairs and post-repair trials and calibrations during the first week in July. On 6 July, *Adams* put to sea for exercises off Santa Catalina and entered port at San Diego on the 10th. After brief post-repair shakedown training and inspections, the destroyer minelayer stood out of San Diego on 17 July on her way back to Hawaii. She arrived at Oahu on the 23rd and spent the next 11 days in gunnery exercises- both antiaircraft and shore bombardment- in the Hawaiian operating area.

On 4 August, *Adams* and *Koiner* (DE-331) departed Pearl Harbor, bound for the western Pacific. The two warships stopped overnight on the 11th and 12th at Eniwetok Atoll where they picked up *Sitka* (APA-113). They escorted the attack transport to the Marianas and arrived at Guam on the 15 August, the day hostilities ceased. The following day, *Adams* got underway for Okinawa , arrived in Buckner Bay on 18 August, and remained there through the 31st. On 1 September, *Adams* stood out of Buckner Bay on her way to Japan. She arrived off Kagoshima, Kyushu, on the 3rd and began sweeping a channel into the port. That operation continued until 9 September at which time *Adams* headed back toward Okinawa. She reached Buckner Bay on 11 September and remained at anchor until the 16th. On that day *Adams* put to sea to evade a typhoon but returned to port on the 18th.

Adams departed Okinawa again on 24 September ; headed for Japan; arrived in Ise Wan, Honshu, on the 26th; and began minesweeping operations in preparation for the landing of Army troops at Nagoya. She anchored in Ise Wan on the 28th and remained there while her commanding officer , double-hatted as task group commander, directed the minesweeping mission. *Adams* remained at Ise Wan through the end of October. On 1 November , the destroyer minelayer laid a course for Sasebo where she arrived two days latter. She stayed there through most of November provisioning ship from units preparing to return home.

On 25 November, *Adams* left Sasebo to voyage to Kiirun, Taiwan, where she arrived on the 28th and reported for duty with Task Group (TG) 70.5. *Adams* returned to sea with TG 70.5 on 4 December for a 10-day minesweeping assignment in Taiwan Strait. At the conclusion of that mission, she returned to Kiirun on 15 December. Four days later, *Adams* put to sea with a convoy bound for Shanghai, China, and entered the Yangtze River on the 21st. *Adams* remained at Shanghai until 3 January 1946. Between 3 and 6 January, the warship voyaged back to Sasebo where she rejoined the 5th Fleet.

Adams continued similar duty in Far Eastern waters until early April when she headed back to the United States. Upon her arrival home, she was assigned to the 1st Fleet and served in it until decommissioned in December. The destroyer minelayer was berthed with the San Diego Group, Pacific Reserve Fleet. *Adams* remained in reserve for almost 23 years. On 7 February 1955, while still in reserve, she was redesignated a fast minelayer MMD-27. Her name was finally struck from the Navy list on 1 December 1970, and *Adams* was sold to Chow's Iron & Steel co., of Taiwan, on 16 December 1971.

Adams (DM-27) earned one battle star for World War II service.

Charles Edward Tolman

United States Naval Academy   Class of 1925

Charles E. Tolman was born on 25 June 1903 in Concord Mass. entered the United States Naval Academy in the summer of 1921 and graduated on 4 June 1925. He was promoted to Lieutenant jg on 4 June 1928 ; Lieutenant, 1 June 1935 ; Lieutenant Commander, 1 August 1939; and Commander (temporary) on 1 August 1942.

After serving in battleship *Utah* (BB-31) , he was transferred to *Worden* (DD-288) in 1926. In 1927 Tolman then completed training courses at the Naval Torpedo Station , Newport, R.I., and at the Submarine Base, New London, Conn. He served in submarines USS *O-4* in 1928 and USS *S-22* from 1929 to 1932 when he returned to the Naval Academy for two years. Tolman served in submarine USS *S-46* in 1934 and commanded USS *S-30* from April 1935 to May 1937. He was attached to the Office of the Chief of Naval Operations for 17 months before assuming command of USS *Spearfish* (SS-190) on 7 October 1939. In January 1941, Tolman joined the staff of Commander, Submarines, Atlantic Fleet.

Commander Tolman became the commanding officer of USS *De Haven* (DD-469) upon her commissioning on 21 September 1942. The destroyer steamed to the South Pacific in November 1942 and supported operations in the Solomons. On the afternoon of 1 February 1943, while escorting landing craft, *De Haven* was attacked by eight Japanese dive bombers. Fighting off the attackers , the destroyer splashed three enemy planes before a bomb struck her navigating bridge, stopped her , and killed Comdr. Tolman. Two more hits and a near miss doomed *De Haven* , which sank within two minutes. Commander Tolman held the American Defense Service Medal with Fleet Clasp; the Asiatic-Pacific Area Campaign Medal ; the Purple Heart ; and the Navy Cross.

National Archives

USS TOLMAN (DM-28)

(DM-28 : dp. 2,200 ; l. 376'6" ; b. 40'10" ; dr. 18'10" ; s. 34.2 ; (tl.) ; cpl. 363 ; a. 6 5", 12 40mm; cl. *Robert H. Smith*)

USS *Tolman* was laid down as hull # 740 on 10 April, 1944 at the Bath Irown Works, Bath, Maine. Reclassified as (DM-28) destroyer minelayer June, 1944 ; launched on 13 August ; sponsored by Mrs. Helen Tolman ; and commissioned on 27 October 1944, Commander Clifford A. Johnson in command. The minelayer had her shakdown off Bermuda during November and December and returned, via Norfolk, to Boston. On 13 January, 1945, *Tolman* departed Boston, MA escorting the USS *Pittsburgh* (CA-72) to the west coast. She called on San Diego on the 27th and then escorted *Birmingham* (CL-62) on to Pearl Harbor. *Tolman* participated in exercises in Hawaii until 23 February and then proceeded to Eniwetok and Ulithi. On 19 March, *Tolman* sortied from Ulithi with Task Group 52.4 to provide fire support and antisubmarine screening for the minesweepers clearing channels prior to the amphibious assault on the Ryukyus. On 22 March, *Tolman*, began clearing the approaches to the beaches of Okinawa.

Shortly after midnight on 28 March, *Tolman* encountered eight Japanese torpedo boats and when they were within 4,000 yards, she opened fire with her five inch guns and forty millimeter batteries. *Tolman* increased her speed to 34 knots and maneuvered radically to avoid the torpedoes. Two of the enemy boats exploded and sank as the remainder laid down a smoke screen. *Tolman* briefly lost contact, but used radar-control fire against the remaining boats, and fired star shells to ferret them out. The last boat was seen to slow, apparently in trouble, just before it was blown up. The ship evidently made a clean sweep of the torpedo boats as a search revealed nothing, and no boats had been seen leaving the area.

Late in the morning of 28 March, 1945, *Tolman* was 500 yards from the USS *Skylark* (AM-63) when *Skylark* struck and detonated a mine against her hull. As *Tolman* maneuvered in to pass a tow line to the stricken ship, *Skylark* hit a second mine and began to settle rapidly. *Tolman* backed down to avoid the mine field and her boats together with PC-1228 and PC-1179 rescued 105 survivors off the stricken *Skylark*. Seven crewmembers aboard *Skylark* were killed and thirty five were wounded.

On 29 March during several heavy air attacks, *Tolman* reported splashing one plane out of three that were attacking the invasion force, one of two in the second attack, and with the aid of *Barton* (DD-722) and *Wiley* (DM-29), two of three in a third. Later in the day *Tolman* shot down a kamikaze that was approaching her in a suicide dive. *Tolman* then proceeded to Kerama Retto to transfer the survivors of the *Skylark* to the other ships.

On the morning of 30 March, *Tolman* encountered three enemy torpedo boats at a range of 3,000 yards. Going to flank speed and made a hard turn to port. One torpedo passed astern and another was reported off her starboard bow. One exploded just off her fantail causing considerable vibration. On 3 April, *Tolman* screened Transport Division 17 to a waiting area 150 miles off Okinawa and remained there for 10 days before returning to the Hagushi beaches.

Tolman grounded on Nagunna Reef off Okinawa on 19 April and remained aground until the 25th. Two tugs then pulled her free and the *Clamp* (ARS-33), a salvage vessel, towed her to Kerama Retto for repairs. *Tolman* entered dry dock on 15 May and was not ready for sea until late in June.

On 28 June, 1945, *Tolman* was underway to the United States. After arriving at San Pedro, California on 21 July, she completed permanent repairs on 8 November and then left for the Far East in early December. *Tolman* arrived in Sasebo the day after Christmas, 1945 and operated out of that port until February, 1946 when *Tolman* shifted her base of operations to Pusan, Korea. She operated out of that port for three months and returned to the United States on 4 May, 1946. *Tolman* was reclassified a fast minelayer (MMD-28) in January, 1969. Proceeding down the coast to San Diego in January 1947, she was decommissioned on the 28th. *Tolman* was struck from the Navy List on 1 December, 1970 and sold for scrapping.

Tolman (DM-28) splashed three enemy aircraft and earned one battle star for World War II service

Henry A. Wiley

United States Naval Academy   Class of 1888

Henry Aristo Wiley was born in Pike County, Ala., 31 January 1867 and graduated from the Naval Academy in 1888. He served in *Maple* during the Spanish-American War and attained his first command, *Villalobos,* in 1904. During the First World War Wiley commanded battleship *Wyoming* attached to the 6th Battle Squadron of the British Grand Fleet and received the Distinguished Service Medal for his outstanding performance. After various shore and fleet commands, he was appointed Admiral in 1927 and served as Commander-in -Chief, U.S. Fleet, until his retirement in 1929 after over 40 years of service. Admiral Wiley served in the years that followed as Chairman of the Maritime Commission and in other important government posts until being recalled to active duty in 1941. In the next year he headed the Navy Board of Production Awards. Admiral Wiley retired once more 2 January 1943 and died 20 May 1943 at Palm Beach, Fla.

69

USS HENRY A. WILEY (DM-29)

(DM-29 : dp 2,200 ; l. 376'5" ; b. 41' ; dr. 15'8" ; s 34k. ; cpl 363 ; a. 6 5" , 8 20mm. ;
cl. *Robert H. Smith*)

Henry A. Wiley (DM-29) was laid down 28 November 1943 as DD-749 by Bethlehem Steel
Co., Staten Island , N.Y.,; launched 21 April 1944 ; sponsored by Mrs. Elizabeth W. Robb,
daughter of Admiral Henry A. Wiley ; reclassified as DM-29, destroyer minelayer 20 July 1944
and commissioned 31 August 1944, Comdr. R.E. Gadrow in command.

After shakedown in the Caribbean, the new minelayer rendezvoused with the battleships *Texas*
BB-35, A*rkansas* and *Missouri* BB-63 and sailed 8 November for the Pacific to earn her nickname
"Hammering Hank." *Henry A. Wiley* reached Pearl Harbor 9 December to prepare for the
impending Iwo Jima campaign. As escort to the battleship *New York* BB-34, she rendezvoused
with other ships of the Gun Fire and Covering Force off the rocky Japanese island 16 February
1945, 3 days before the initial landings. She remained there until 9 March, to provide fire support
and screen ships often operating a mere 400 yards from Mount Suribachi. The minelayer poured
some 3,600 rounds into the Japanese fortress.

A second and even more arduous campaign followed for *Henry A. Wiley* - Okinawa, the largest
amphibious operation of the Pacific War. Reaching her position 23 March, D-day minus eight, she
began to screen minesweepers as they cleared channels for transports and support ships. Japanese

resistance was fierce and air attacks were almost unceasing. On 28 March *Henry A. Wiley* splashed two kamikazes, and the next morning in 15 hectic minutes saw a bomb explode 50 yards astern, downed two more kamikazes, and rescued a downed fighter pilot. While screening transports on 1 April, D-day at Okinawa, *Henry A. Wiley* destroyed her fifth kamikaze.

The battle-tried ship then shifted to radar picket duty and spent a total of 34 days on this important task alerting other ships of enemy air attacks. In this period *Henry A. Wiley* took 64 enemy aircraft under fire, destroying several. The morning of 4 May proved especially eventful. She began by splashing a Betty at 0307. When her sister ship *Luce* DD-522 was hit by two kamikazes and reported sinking, *Henry A. Wiley* proceeded to her aid, but came under heavy air attack. In less than a quarter hour of heavy fighting, the valiant ship splashed three kamikazes and two Baka bombers, one of which was closing from the starboard quarter when it was hit by *Henry A. Wiley's* accurate fire. It hit the water, bounced over the fantail, and exploded just off the port quarter. Having expended nearly 5,000 rounds of 5 inch and AA ammunition, the minelayer then proceeded to rescue survivors from *Luce* which sank at 0740 with the loss of 126 of her crew. For her intreipid actions of Okinawa, which resulted in the destruction of 15 Japanese airplanes, *Henry A. Wiley* received the coveted Presidential Unit Citation, and her skipper the Navy Cross and Legion of Merit.

From Okinawa *Henry A. Wiley* sailed for the East China Sea, entering 12 June to screen minesweepers attempting to clear that vast body of water. She remained on this duty, with brief respites at Buckner Bay, until peace came. Even this was ushered in to the sound of "Hammering Hanks" guns, as on the night of 14 August, 24 hours before final orders to cease offensive operations against the Japanese were received, she went to General Quarters 6 times at the approach of enemy aircraft, finally opening fire on the 6th run as an attack run was commenced. *Henry A. Wiley* remained in the Pacific to screen and guide minesweepers through the end of 1945. She streamed her homeward bound pennant 17 January 1946 and on 7 February reached San Francisco via Eniwetok and Pearl Harbor. *Henry A. Wiley* decommissioned at San Francisco 29 January 1947 and went into reserve at San Diego into 1967. *Henry A. Wiley* was sold for scrapping 15 October 1970.

Henry A. Wiley was credited with 15 enemy aircraft and 2 Baka bombers, in addition to the Presidential Unit Commendation, received four battle stars for her participation in World War II.

National Archives

John Joseph Shea

John Joseph Shea, born in Cambridge, Mass., on 13 January 1898, enlisted in the Naval Reserve Force on 11 June 1918. At the time of his release from active duty in 1919, he was promoted to the rank of ensign. He was honorably discharged in 1921 and reappointed in 1923. With the abolition of the Naval Reserve Force in 1925, he was transferred to the Fleet Reserve. In 1941, he was transferred to the Regular Navy in the rank of lieutenant commander. Lt. Comdr. Shea was serving in *Wasp* (CV-7) on 15 September 1942, when she was torpedoed and sunk by the Japanese.

He left the relative safety of his own station to direct the fight against the raging inferno on *Wasp's* flight deck. Amid frequent explosions and flying debris, he worked to save the carrier. He was leading out another hose to continue the struggle against the fires in a ready ammunition room when a shattering explosion occurred. In all probability, Lt. Comdr. Shea died in that explosion; but, lacking concrete proof of death, he was declared Missing in Action until a year and a day latter when he was declared legally dead. Shea was awarded the Navy Cross and Purple Heart medals and was promoted to commander, all posthumously.

National Archives

USS SHEA (DM-30)

(DM-30 : dp 2,200 ; l. 376'6" ; b. 40'0" ; dr. 18'8" ; s. 34.2 k.; cpl. 363 ; a. 6 5" , 10 40mm. ; cl. *Robert H. Smith*)

Shea , a destroyer minelayer , was laid down on 23 December 1943 by Bethlehem Steel Co. yard at Staten Island, N.Y., as DD-750, an *Allen M. Sumner* class destroyer ; launched on 20 May 1944 : sponsored by Mrs. John J. Shea ; modified to be a destroyer minelayer and reclassified DM-30 in June 1944 ; and commissioned at the New York Navy Yard on 30 September 1944 , Comdr. Charles C. Kirkpatrick in command.

Shea spent 15 more days completing her fitting-out. She then loaded ammunition at Earle and Bayonne, N.J., returned briefly to New York and departed for her shakedown cruise on 21 October 1944. She completed shakedown training at and around Great Sound Bay, Bermuda, and was underway for Norfolk, Va., on 16 November. *Shea's* crew underwent a month of further training in the Norfolk area before embarking, 13 December , for Brooklyn, N.Y., arriving the next day.

From Brooklyn *Shea* moved on to San Francisco Bay, California. Sailing with TG 27.3 she transited the Panama canal 20-22 December and made San Francisco on the last day of 1944. Four days later , she was underway for Pearl Harbor, Hawaii, and 13 more days of training exercises. Another round of training completed, she steamed out of Pearl Harbor bound for Eniwetok Atoll in the western Pacific, arriving 2 March. After 17 days in the vicinity of Eniwetok, her crew engaged in still more of the perennial training exercises. *Shea* departed for Ulithi Atoll on the first leg of her cruise into the real war at Okinawa.

On 19 March 1945, she sailed from Ulithi and joined TG 52.3. By 24 March, *Shea* was off Okinawa helping prepare the way for the 1 April invasion. While her primary mission was to protect and assist the minesweepers clearing the area of enemy mines, she also stood radar picket duty all around Okinawa. During the period 24 March-4 May, she was constantly fending off Japanese air attacks and guarding against enemy submarines. Moreover, she probably sank or severely damaged at least one submarine and, on 16 April, in the space of 10 minutes, splashed no less than six enemy planes.

On the morning of 4 May 1945, *Shea* was en route to radar picket duty 20 miles NE of Zampa Misaki, Okinawa. She arrived just after 0600, having encountered two Japanese aircraft along the way, firing on both and possibly splashing one. Upon receipt of reports indicating the approach of large Japanese air formations, *Shea*'s crew went to General Quarters. Soon thereafter , a " considerable smoke haze blew over the ship from the Hagushi beaches " and " visibility was at a maximum 5,000 yards ." At 0854 a single enemy Betty was sighted six miles distant ; and, four minutes later. one was shot down by *Shea*- directed CAP. At 0859, five minutes after the initial sighting, a lookout spotted a Japanese *baka* bomb on *Shea's* starboard beam, closing the ship at better than 450 knots. Almost instantaneously, the *baka* crashed *Shea* " on the starboard side of her bridge structure, entering the sonar room, traversing the chart house, passageway and hatch, and exploding beyond the port side on the surface of the water. Fire broke out in the mess hall, CIC, chart house, division commander's stateroom, #2 upper handling room, and compartment A304-L"

Shea lost all ships communications. 5" gun mounts numbers 1 and 2 were inoperative ; and the forward port 20 millimeter guns were damaged. The main director was jammed and the gyro and computer rendered unserviceable. One officer and 26 men were killed, and 91 others were wounded to varying degrees.

With repair parties and survivors from damaged areas scurrying about, helping the wounded and fighting fires, *Shea*, listing 5 degrees to port, began limping off to Hagushi and medical assistance. She arrived there at 1052 ; her most seriously wounded crew members were transferred to *Crescent City* (APA-21) ; and the bodies of the 27 dead were removed for burial on Okinawa. *Shea* then resumed her limping, this time to Kerama Retto anchorage. At Kerama Retto, she underwent repairs and disgorged all but 10 percent of her ammunition. In addition, much of her gear, particularly radar and fighter direction equipment, was transferred to DesRon 2 for distribution to less severely damaged ships. After a memorial service on 11 May for her dead crewmen and the removal of some armament, *Shea* was underway on 15 May to join convoy OKU #4 (TU 51.29.9), heading for Ulithi Atoll.

Shea got underway from Ulithi on 27 May 1945 and, after a three-day layover at Pearl Harbor, departed for Philadelphia on 9 June. She arrived at the Philadelphia Navy Yard on 2 July, visiting San Diego and transiting the Panama Canal en route. *Shea* underwent extensive repairs and post-repair trails before leaving Philadelphia on 11 October for shakedown at Casco Bay, Maine. While in the area, *Shea* celebrated her first peacetime Navy Day at Bath, Maine.

From 1946 to late 1953, *Shea* was engaged in normal operations with the Atlantic Fleet. Assigned to MinDiv 2 and based at Charleston, S.C., she ranged the Atlantic seaboard and Caribbean Sea. This employment was interrupted late in 1950 by a Mediterranean cruise, during which she visited Trieste on a liaison mission with the British forces in the area. *Shea* returned to Charleston and the Atlantic Fleet on 1 February 1951 and remained so engaged until September 1953 when she re-entered the Pacific.

Shea spent the remainder of her active service in the Pacific, based at Long Beach, California. She participated in numerous minelaying and antisubmarine exercises off the west coast, covering the area from Mexico north to British Columbia and west to Hawaii. In the spring of 1954, she made her only excursion out of that area when she took part in the atomic tests conducted at Eniwetok Atoll in the Marshall Islands. This was her first and only return to any of her old World War II haunts. She arrived back in Long Beach on 28 May and remained in the area until 9 April 1958 when she was placed out of commission in reserve. *Shea* continued in this reserve status until 1 September at which time , after being surveyed and deemed not to be up to fleet standards, she was stricken from the Navy list.

Shea (DM-30) earned one battle star in the Okinawa Campaign and was awarded the Navy Unit Citation during World War II.

Library of Congress

J. William Ditter

J. William Ditter was born in Philadelphia 5 September 1888. He received a law degree from Temple University Law School in 1913, following which he taught in the Philadelphia public schools and practiced law. Ditter was selected to Congress from the 17th District of Pennsylvania in 1932, and during his years in Washington served on the House Committee on Appropriations. He also was a member of the subcommittee on Navy Department appropriation bills, and at the time of his death was ranking minority member. Congressman Ditter was a supporter of a strong Navy and vitally interested in its welfare. He was killed in an airplane crash near Lancaster, Pa., 21 November 1943.

National Archives

J. WILLIAM DITTER (DM-31)

(DM-31 : dp. 2,200 ; l. 376'5" ; b. 14' ; dr. 15'8" ; s. 34k.; cpl. 336 ; a. 6 5", 8 20mm., 4dcp ., 2dct. ; cl. *Robert H. Smith*)

J. William Ditter (DM-31) was laid down as DD-751 on 25 January 1944 by the Bethlehem Shipbuilding Co., Staten Island, N.Y. ; was launched 4 July 1944 ; sponsored by Mrs. J. William Ditter, widow of Congressman Ditter ; reclassified DM-31 19 July 1944 ; and commissioned at New York Navy Yard 28 October 1944, Comdr. R.R. Sampson in command.

J. William Ditter completed her shakedown off Bermuda in December. She sailed from Norfolk 13 January 1945, and after transiting the Panama Canal and touching at San Diego arrived Pearl Harbor 10 February.

As the Navy's island-hopping thrust toward Japan reached its climax, *J. William Ditter* sailed 2 March for Eniwetok and Ulithi, departing the latter base 19 March for Okinawa. She arrived 25 March off the critical island , soon to be the largest scene of the largest amphibious assault of the Pacific war, and began hazardous minesweeping operations. The next day *Ditter* dodged a torpedo during an encounter with a Japanese submarine. On 29 March she discovered two suicide boats off Okinawa, and sank one of them with gunfire. By the day of the invasion, 1 April, *J. William Ditter* and her sister minecraft had swept the channels and laid marker buoys, contributing importantly to the success of the initial landing. Next day her duties shifted to convoy escort, as the versatile ship protected transports on night retirement away from Okinawa. On the night of 2 April the ship shot down two bombers, and she continued to come under air attack in the days that followed as the Japanese made a desperate but futile effort to stop the invasion with kamikaze tactics.

J. William Ditter was assigned radar picket duty 12 April, and, subsequently, became the target of heavy air attack. She shot down several planes and assisted with several more until retiring to Kerama Retto 30 April. The ship was soon back on picket duty , however, and engaged in numerous battles with Japanese aircraft. While patrolling with *Harry F. Bauer* (DM-26) and *Ellyson* (DD-454) 6 June, *J. William Ditter* was attacked by a large group of kamikazes. The ship's gun crews downed five of the planes ; but a sixth glanced off her No. 2 stack ; and another crashed her on the port side near the main deck.

The ship lost all power and suffered many casualties ; but valiant damage control kept her afloat until she could be towed by fleet tug *Ute* to Kerama Retto next day. Eventually she was repaired enough to steam to Saipan 10 July and began the long voyage home. She touched at San Diego and the Canal Zone before arriving New York 12 July 1945. *J. William Ditter* decommissioned there 28 September 1945 and was scrapped in July 1946.

J. William Ditter (DM-31) received one battle star for World War II service

Naval Institute

Eugene E. Lindsey

United States Naval Academy   Class of 1927

Eugene E. Lindsey, born in Sprague, Washington, 2 July 1905, graduated from the Naval Academy in 1927. After duty in *Nevada* (BB-36) and *Saratoga* (CV-3) he completed flight training in 1929, and served with a bombing squadron in *Lexington* (CV-2) and an observation squadron in *Maryland* (BB-46). From 3 June 1940 he commanded a torpedo squadron in *Enterprise* (CV-6) .

Lindsey was awarded the Distinguished Flying Cross for brilliantly successful leadership of his squadron in attacks on Kwajalein and Wotje in the Marshalls 1 February 1942. He gave his life in action 4 June 1942 in the Battle of Midway, in which his squadron played a valiant and selfless role, pressing home their attack through merciless antiaircraft fire. He was posthumously awarded the Navy Cross for his important contribution to this great American victory.

USS LINDSEY (DM-32)   National Archives

(DM-32 : dp. 2,200 ; l. 376'6"" ; b. 40'10" ; dr. 18'10" ; s. 34k. ; cpl 363 ; a. 6 5", 12 40mm.; cl. *Robert* H. Smith)

Lindsey (DM-32) was laid down as DD-771 12 September 1943 by Bethlehem Steel Co., San Pedro, California; launched 5 March 1944; sponsored by Mrs. Eugene E. Lindsey, widow of Lt. Comdr. Lindsey; reclassified (DM-32) destroyer minelayer 19 July 1944; and commissioned 20 August 1944, Comdr. T.E. Chambers in command.

After shakedown off southern California the new destroyer minelayer sailed from San Francisco 25 November 1944 via Pearl Harbor for Ulithi, arriving 3 February 1945. Underway from Ulithi the morning of 8 February, *Lindsey* steamed toward Iwo Jima. Operating off Iwo Jima 17 to 19 February, *Lindsey* knocked out six enemy guns ashore and provided covering fire as minesweepers cleared the harbor. On the 23rd she returned to Ulithi to prepare for landings on Okinawa.

Underway 19 March, *Lindsey* arrived off Okinawa 24 March and swept the harbor for the inbound transports. Then as marines gained a foothold, the ship bombarded Japanese gun installations and transferred wounded soldiers to hospital ships. On the afternoon of 12 April, *Lindsey* experienced a mass kamikaze attack. Her gunners scored repeated hits on seven onrushing dive bombers, but two " Vals " , damaged and out of control, crashed *Lindsey* killing 57 sailors and wounding 57 more. The explosion from the second " Val " ripped some 60 feet off her bow. Only the " all back full " ordered by Commander Chambers prevented the pressure of inrushing water from collapsing the fireroom bulkhead and sinking the ship.

Towed to Kerama Retto the same night, *Lindsey* remained in the lagoon for 2 weeks repairing battle damage. On 28 April she departed under tow for Guam where, after arrival 6 May, *Lindsey* received a temporary bow. She sailed under her own power 8 July for the east coast via Pearl Harbor and the Panama Canal, arriving Norfolk 19 August 1945.

After extensive repairs at the Norfolk Naval Shipyard, *Lindsey* steamed 6 March 1946 for Charleston, S.C., and arrived the next day. *Lindsey* decommissioned 25 May 1946 and entered the Atlantic Reserve Fleet. She is berthed at Philadelphia into 1969. *Lindsey* was stricken from the Navy list as of 1 October 1970 and sold for scrapping.

Lindsey (DM-32) received two battle stars for World War II service.

Naval Historical Center

William Gwin

William Gwin was born 6 December 1832 in Columbus, Ind., and appointed a Midshipman 7 April 1847. Passed 19 June 1853. Master 15 September 1855. Lieutenant 16 September 1855. Lt. Commander 16 July 1862. One of the most promising officers in the nation, he had risen to the rank of Lieutenant Commander by the time of his death. During the Civil War he commanded several ships of the Mississippi Squadron. He was one of Flag Officer Foote's "can do" officers, displaying outstanding initiative, energy and dash. After the fall of Fort Henry he swept with his wooden gunboats up the Tennessee River all the way to regions of Alabama, spreading destruction and terror. This action was a major factor in the collapse of the Confederate lines far behind him in Kentucky. Fire support from two of his gunboats, *Tyler and Lexington,* helped save Union troops from disaster in the Battle of Shiloh, bringing high praise from General Grant. He was wounded in action 27 December 1862 while commanding gunboat *Benton* in the battle of Haines Bluff on the Yazoo River. He died from these injuries 3 January 1863 on board a hospital ship in the Mississippi River.

engraved by J.C. Buttre, New York

National Archives

USS GWIN (DM-33)

(DM-33 : dp. 2,200 ; l. 376'6" ; b. 40'10" ; dr. 18'10" ; s. 34.2 k. ; cpl 343 ; a. 6 5", 12 40mm., 8 20mm., 2 dct., 4 dep. ; cl. *Robert H. Smith*)

Gwin (DM-33) was laid down 31 October 1943 as DD-772 ; was launched by Bethlehem Steel Co., San Pedro, Calif., 9 April 1944 : sponsored by Mrs. Jesse W. Tarbill, second cousin and sponsor of the previous *Gwin* (DD-433) ; reclassified DM-33 destroyer minelayer June 1944 ; and commissioned 30 September 1944 at Los Angeles, Comdr. F.S. Steinke in command.

After shakedown along the California coast, *Gwin* sailed for the Pacific theater as flagship of Mine Squadron 3, reaching Pearl Harbor 3 January 1945. A week later the squadron left for the fighting front. At Saipan, 20 January, *Gwin* and her sister sweepers joined Battleship Division 7. For 7 days, 21 to 26 January, she participated in the preliminary bombardment of Iwo Jima, next to the last step in America's long island-hopping campaign across the Pacific. Returning to Pearl Harbor, *Gwin* underwent overhaul before sailing for Eniwetok 23 February.

From Eniwetok *Gwin* steamed to Nansei Shoto 17 March to sweep the area around Okinawa, the scene of one of the war's bloodiest and most heroic invasions. Acting in a variety of roles-antisubmarine screen, radar picket ship, minesweeper, fire support-*Gwin* was to remain off Okinawa the following 5 months, almost to the very end of the war. During this period she accounted for some 16 enemy aircraft as the Japanese launched their desperate kamikaze attacks. Nine of these Japanese planes fell victim to *Gwin's* guns on only 2 days, 16 April and 4 May. An air raid 16 April saw *Gwin* down two "Betties", Japanese dive bombers, coming in only to have another come sweeping in and crash in the sea some 25 yards as the agile DM evaded her. And then the alert gun crew swung their battery to catch another Japanese plane and shoot it down less than 50 yards from the ship.

At dusk on 4 May, *Gwin* was on radar picket station off Okinawa. CAP (Combat Air Patrol) reported 8 to 10 enemy planes to port, and *Gwin* swung her batteries to face the enemy. Suddenly a second contingent of planes swept in out of the setting sun to starboard! *Gwin* swung her guns around just in time , and two of the attackers splashed into the sea. Whirling to port, the gun crews fired into the original attack group, and accounted for three more kamikazes. The seas had not yet closed over these three planes when a sixth, another kamikaze, crashed *Gwin*. Two men were killed, 2 missing, and 11 injured as the suicide plane embedded itself into *Gwin's* aft 40 mm. platform. Then as damage control parties rushed to quell the fires raging around the kamikaze, the Japanese attack ended as suddenly as it had begun. In less than six hectic, heroic minutes, *Gwin*, although under attack from all quarters, had downed five Japanese planes and been herself damaged by a sixth.

After a brief stay at Nansei Shoto for battle damage repairs *Gwin* returned to patrol and sweeping duties around Okinawa. She rendezvoused 20 August with Task Force 38 and, with such illustrious fighting ships as *Missouri, Lexington, Yorktown, and Shangri-La,* headed for Tokyo Bay. Putting into Sagami Bay 27 August 1945, *Gwin* began to sweep the area, front door to Tokyo Bay , and destroyed some 41 mines in two days duty. At last on 29 August 1945 she steamed into Tokyo Bay, and anchored under the towering snowcap of Mount Fujiyama. Departing for Okinawa 1 September, *Gwin* remained on minesweeping duty there and in the East China Sea for the rest of the year.

With her share of the Pacific "mopping-up" complete, *Gwin* at last headed home, reaching San Pedro, Calif., 23 February 1946. The battle-tested ship then sailed for Charleston, S.C., arriving 14 March. *Gwin* decommissioned there 3 September 1946 and was placed in reserve .

As the Korean War necessitated the strengthening of America's fleet, *Gwin* recommissioned at Charleston 8 July 1952, Comdr. R.E. Oliver in command. For the next few years she divided her time between Caribbean and local exercises, European cruises, and NATO maneuvers, with time out for overhaul. In 1953 *Gwin* crossed the Atlantic for a 4-month tour of duty with the 6th Fleet, visiting 10 Mediterranean ports before returning to Charleston 3 February 1954. Midshipman Able Cruises June to August 1954 and 1955 took her to Lisbon, Portugal, Le Havre Valencia, Spain, and Terquay, England. *Gwin* returned to the Mediterranean a final time in 1957 for NATO maneuvers with ships of the Portugese, French, and British navies, visiting both Brest and Gibraltar.

In between Caribbean and Mediterranean cruises and training, *Gwin* engaged in a variety of minesweeping and hunter-killer antisubmarine exercises along the East Coast and participated in several other NATO maneuvers in American waters. *Gwin* sailed to the Philadelphia Navy Yard 12 January 1958 where she decommissioned 3 April 1958 and remains in reserve through 1967.

On 22 October 1971 as " MAUVENET " D-357 was under the flag of Turkey. Ancient *Gwin* , in her 49th year serving with the Turkish Navy as " *Mauvenet* " met her end when USS Saratoga accidentally placed two missiles into her bridge.

Gwin was credited with 16 enemy planes, received a Navy Unit Commendation and four battle stars for service in World War II.

Naval Institute

Aaron Ward

United States Naval Academy   Class of 1871

Born in Philadelphia 10 October 1851, Aaron Ward graduated from the Academy in 1871. He commanded *Wasp* in Cuban waters during April - September 1898. Commended for gallantry, he was advanced to Lieutenant Commander for conspicuous service at the Battle of Santiago. He commanded the 3rd Division, Atlantic Fleet, 1911-12, and served as Supervisor of New York Harbor until retired 10 October 1913. Rear Admiral Ward died in Roslyn, N.Y., 5 July 1918 and is buried in Greenwood Cemetery, Brooklyn, N.Y.

National Archives

Aaron Ward (DM-34)

(DM-34 : dp. 2200 ; l. 376' 6" ; b. 40'10" ; dr. 18'10" ; s. 34.2k. ; cpl. 363 ; a. 6 5" ; cl. *Robert H. Smith*)

Aaron Ward (DM-34) a destroyer minelayer converted from an *Allen M. Sumner* class destroyer hull ; was laid down as DD-773 on 12 December 1943 at San Pedro, Calif., by the Bethlehem Steel Corp. ; launched on 5 May 1945 ; sponsored by Mrs. G.H. Ratliff ; redesignated a destroyer minelayer, DM-34 on 19 July 1944 ; and placed in commission on 28 October 1944, Comdr. William H. Sanders Jr. , in command.

Between commissioning and the end of January 1945, *Aaron Ward* completed fitting out and conducted her shakedown cruise off the California coast. On 9 February, she departed San Pedro , bound for Pearl Harbor where she arrived on 15 February. The warship conducted additional training in Hawaiian waters before loading supplies and ammunition and getting underway on 5 March to join the 5th Fleet at Ulithi. She entered the lagoon of that atoll in the Western Carolines on 16 March but put to sea on the 19th with Task Force (TF) 52 bound for the Ryukyu Islands.

The Mine Flotilla, of which *Aaron Ward* was a unit, arrived off Okinawa late on 22nd. The following day, the destroyer minelayer got her first glimpse of the enemy when some of his planes approached the sweep group but did not attack. More came in later, but the combine gunfire of the group dissuaded them from approaching close enough to harm the American ships. The first actual air raid occurred on the 26th, and the *Adams* (DM-27) knocked the intruder out of the sky.

Aaron Ward supported minesweeping operations around Kerama Retto and Okinawa until the time of the first landings. During that period ; she accounted for three enemy aircraft. On 1 April, the day of the initial assault on Okinawa , the destroyer minelayer began screening the heavy warships providing gunfire support for the troops ashore. The duty lasted until 4 April when she departed Ryukyus and headed for the Marianas. She arrived at Saipan on the 10th but shifted to Guam later that day. After several days of minor repairs, *Aaron Ward* headed back to Okinawa to patrol in the area around Kerama Retto. During that patrol period, she came under frequent air attack. On the 27th, she splashed one enemy plane and , the next day, accounted for one more and claimed a probable kill in addition . She returned to Kerama Retto to replenish her provisions and fuel. While she was there , a kamikaze scored a hit on *Pinkney* (APH-2). *Aaron Ward* moved alongside the stricken evacuation transport to help fight the inferno blazing admidships. While so engaged, she also rescued 12 survivors from *Pinkney.*

On 30 April, the destroyer minelayer returned to sea to take up position on radar picket station number 10. That night, she helped repulse several air attacks ; but for the most part, weather kept enemy airpower away until the afternoon of 3 May. when the weather began to clear, the probability of air attacks rose. At dusk, *Aaron Ward's* radar picked up bogies at 27 miles distance ; and her crew went to general quarters. Two of the planes in the formation broke away and began run on *Aaron Ward.* The warship opened fire on the first from about 7,000 yards and began scoring hits when he had closed the range to 4,000 yards. At that point, he dipped over into his suicide dive but splashed about 100 yards off the destroyer minelayer's starboard quarter. The second of the pair began his approach immediately thereafter. *Aaron Ward* opened fire on him at about 8,000 yards and, once again, began scoring hits to good effect, so much so that her antiaircraft battery destroyed him while he was still 1,200 yards away.

At that point, a third and more determined intruder appeared and dove in on *Aaron Ward's* stern. Though repeatedly struck by antiaircraft fire, the plane pressed home the attack with grim determination. Just before crashing into *Aaron Ward's* superstructure, he released a bomb which smashed through her hull below the water line and exploded in the after engine room. The bomb explosion flooded the after engine and fire rooms, ruptured fuel tanks, set the leaking oil ablaze, and severed steering control connections to the bridge. The rudder jammed at hard left, and *Aaron Ward* turned in a tight circle while slowing to about 20 knots. Topside, the plane itself spread fire and destruction through the area around the after deckhouse and deprived mount 53 of all power and communication. Worse yet, many sailors were killed or injured in the crash.

For about 20 minutes, no attacking plane succeeded in penetrating her air defenses. Damage control parties worked feverishly to put out fires, to repair what damage they could, to jettison ammunition in danger of exploding, and to attend to the wounded. Though steering control was moved aft to the rudder itself, the ship was unable to maneuver properly throughout the remainder of the engagement. Then, at about 1840, the ships on her station came under a particularly ferocious air attack. While *Little* (DD-803) was hit by the five successive crashes that sank her, *LSMR-* 195 took the crash that sent her to the bottom ; and *LCSL-* 25 lost her mast to a suicider. *Aaron Ward* also suffered her share of added woe. Just before 1900, one plane from the group of attackers selected her as a target and began his approach from about 8,000 yards. Fortunately, the destroyer minelayer began scoring hits early and managed to splash the attacker when he was still 2,000 yards away. Another enemy then attempted to crash into her, but he, too, succumbed to her antiaircraft fire.

Her troubles, however, were not over. Soon after the two successes just mentioned, two more Japanese planes came in on her port bow. Though chased by American fighters, one of these succeeded in breaking away and started a run on *Aaron Ward.* He came in at a steep dive apparently aiming at the bridge. Heavy fire from the destroyer minelayer, however forced him to veer toward the after portion of the ship. Passing over the signal bridge, he carried away halyards and antennae assemblies, smashed into the stack and then splashed down close aboard to starboard.

Quickly on the heels of that attack, still another intruder swooped in toward *Aaron Ward.* Coming in just forward of her port beam, he met a hail of antiaircraft fire but pressed home his attack resolutely and released a bomb just before he crashed into her main deck. The bomb exploded a few feet close aboard her port side, and it's fragments showered the ship and blew a large hole through the shell plating near her forward fireroom. As a result, the ship lost all power and gradually lost headway. At that point, a previously unobserved enemy crashed into the ship's deckhouse bulkhead causing numerous fires and injuring and killing many more crewmen.

As if that were not enough, *Aaron Ward* had to endure two more devastating crashes before the action ended. At about 1921, a plane glided in steeply on her port quarter. The loss of power prevented any of her 5-inch mounts from bearing on him, and he crashed into her port superstructure. Burning gasoline engulfed the deck in flames, 40- millimeter ammunition began exploding, and still more heavy casualties resulted. The warship went dead in the water, her after superstructure deck demolished, and she was still on fire. While damage control crews fought the fires and flooding, *Aaron Ward* began to settle in the water and took on a decided list to port.

She still had one ordeal, however, to suffer. Just after 1920, a final bomb-laden tormentor made a high-speed, low-level approach and crashed into the base of her number 2 stack. The explosion blew the plane, the stack, searchlight, and two gun mounts into the air, and they all came to rest strewn across the deck aft of stack number 1. Through the night, her crew fought to save the ship. At 2106, *Shannon* (DM-25) arrived and took *Aaron Ward* in tow. Early on the morning of 4 May, she arrived at Kerama Retto where she began temporary repairs. She remained there until 11 June when she got under way for the United States. Steaming via Ulithi, Guam, Eniwetok, Pearl Harbor, and the Panama Canal, *Aaron Ward* arrived New York in mid-August. On 28 September, she was decommissioned, and her name struck from the Navy list. In July 1946, she was sold for scrapping.

National Archives

Aaron Ward (DM-34) was hit by six kamikaze planes, earned one battle star and the Presidential Unit Citation for World War II service.

National Archives

<u>USS PALAU (CVE-122)</u>

(Cve-122 ; dp. 11,373 ; l. 557' 1" ; b. 75' ; ew. 105' 5" ; dr. 32' ; s. 19k. ; cpl. 1066; a. 2 5", 36 40mm. ; c. Commencement Bay)

Palau (CVE-122) was laid down by the Todd-Pacific Shipyards Inc., Tacoma, Washington, 19 February 1945; launched 6 August 1945; sponsored by Mrs. J.P. Whitney; and commissioned 15 January 1946, Capt. W.E. Cleaves in command.

Commissioned as the Navy began its post-war demobilization, Palau completed shakedown off California, transited the Panama Canal, underwent post shakedown availability at Boston, and on 11 May moved down the coast to Norfolk where she was immobilized until May 1947. On 22 May she steamed south to Cuba for refresher training, after which she headed north to Norfolk and New York, whence with escorts *Fraser* DM-24 and *Shannon* DM-25, she steamed to Recife, Brazil S.A. thence to West African ports of Monrovia, Liberia and Dakar, French West Africa. She returned to the East coast 16 August and after another Availability at Boston was again immobilized at Norfolk, December 1947 through March 1948. During the spring of 1948 she conducted operations off the east coast and on 3 June departed for the Mediterranean to deliver planes, under the Turkish Aid Program to representatives of that country at Yesilkoy. Returning to Norfolk 7 August, she remained in the western Atlantic, ranging from the Maritine Provinces to the West Indies, until April 1952. Then departing Norfolk, she returned to the Mediterranean to operate with the 6th. Fleet until late June, when she resumed duties with the 2nd. Fleet on the East coast.

Palau, designated for inactivation in early 1953, was retained in commission to preform one final ferry assignment, planes to Yokosuka; 8 August thru 22 October. On her return she entered the Philadelphia Naval Shipyard, decommissioned 15 June 1954. Berthed with the Philadelphia Group, Atlantic Reserve Fleet, Palau remained a unit of that fleet until struck from the Navy List 1 April 1960 and sold for scrap, 13 July 1960, to Jacques Pierot, Jr. and Sons, New York.

National Archives

USS TERROR (CM-5)

(CM-5 : dp. 5,875 ; l. 454' 10" ; b. 60' 2" ; dr. 19' 7" ; s. 20.3 k.; cpl 481 ; a. 4 5", 16 1.1" ,
14 20mm.; cl. *Terror*)

Terror (CM-5) - the Navy's only minelayer built specifically for minelaying - was laid down on
3 September 1940 by the Philadelphia Navy Yard ; launched on 6 June 1941 ; sponsored by Mrs.
Ralph A. Bard ; commissioned on 15 July 1942, Comdr. Howard Wesley Fitch in command.

During the early 50's, she was placed in service in reserve ; and , on 7 February 1955 , she was
redesignated a fleet minelayer (MM-5). Her designation symbol was changed to MMF-5 in
October 1955 , and she was decommissioned on 6 August 1956. In 1971, her hulk was sold to the
Union Minerals and Alloys Corporation, of New York City.

Terror received four battle stars for World War II service.

National Archives

The Mk 6 pictured is but one of four types of mines carried by the Sumner Class Destroyer Minelayers (DM). It is a moored, contact mine which consist of an anchor, spherical case and antenna. The case contains 300 lb. of HBX-1 explosive filler. The mine could be detonated by contact with the antenna or directly with the mine itself. 120 of this type mine could be caried by the Sumner Class destroyers. The mines were stored on tracks which ran down the Port and Starboard side of the ship with a turntable at the quarter deck to transfer mines from one side to the other. A large heavy duty steam winch was mounted on the fantail with its cable anchored to the last mine forward , when pulled would hump the end mine off the fantail. This operation could be conducted while the ship was at high speed.

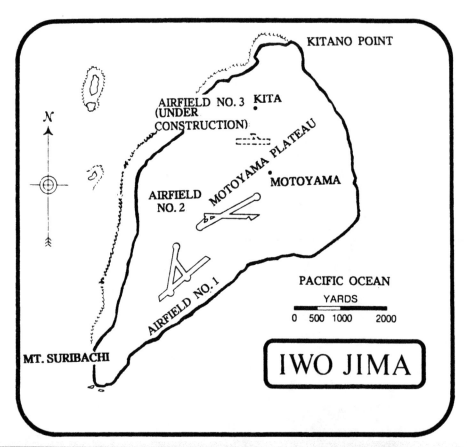

KITANO POINT

AIRFIELD NO. 3 KITA
(UNDER
CONSTRUCTION)

MOTOYAMA PLATEAU

AIRFIELD
NO. 2

MOTOYAMA

AIRFIELD NO. 1

PACIFIC OCEAN

YARDS

0   500 1000   2000

IWO JIMA

MT. SURIBACHI

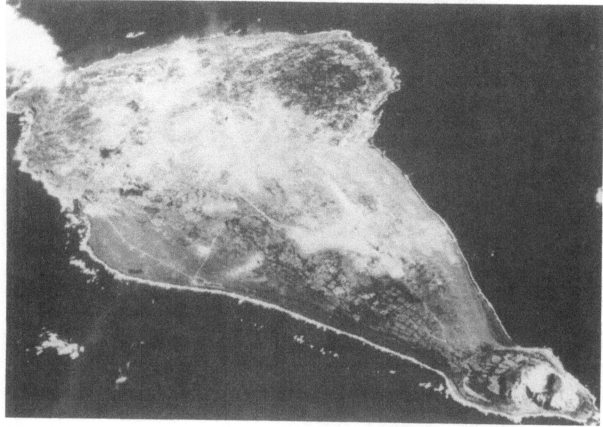

National Archives

17 February 1945
Bombardment of Mt. Suribachi and Iwo Jima. Taken from USS Arkansas (BB-33)
Destroyer Minelayer USS Henry A. Wiley (DM-29) in foreground.

National Archives

17 February 1945
The Destroyer Minelayer USS Henry A.Wiley (DM-29) passes between Iwo Jima and USS Arkansas (BB-33)
in order to get a close range on the island.

National Archives

21 February 1945

USS Henry A. Wiley (DM-29) as seen from USS LCI-648 with Mt. Suribachi " Hot Rock " in background.

National Archives

17 February 1945
Bombardment of Mt. Suribachi and Iwo Jima. Taken from USS Arkansas (BB-33)

OLD GLORY FLIES FROM "HOT ROCKS"

23 February 1945

" At 1030 word was passed over the battle announcing system that the Marines had reached the top of Mt. Suribachi and that " Old Glory " was flying from the summit. By straining our eyes a little bit we not only could distinguish the flag flying but also the small band of Marines that were protecting the site. " (Saga of the Fraser)

National Archives

Re-enactment scene of the flag raising on Mt. Suribachi.

Left to Right : Pfc. Ira H. Hayes; Pfc. Franklin R. Sously, killed in action; Sergeant Michael Strank, killed in action; Pharmacist Mate 2c John H. Bradley; Pfc. Rene A. Gagnon; Corporal Harlon H. Block, killed in action. (Photo by Joe Rosenthal, Associated Press.)

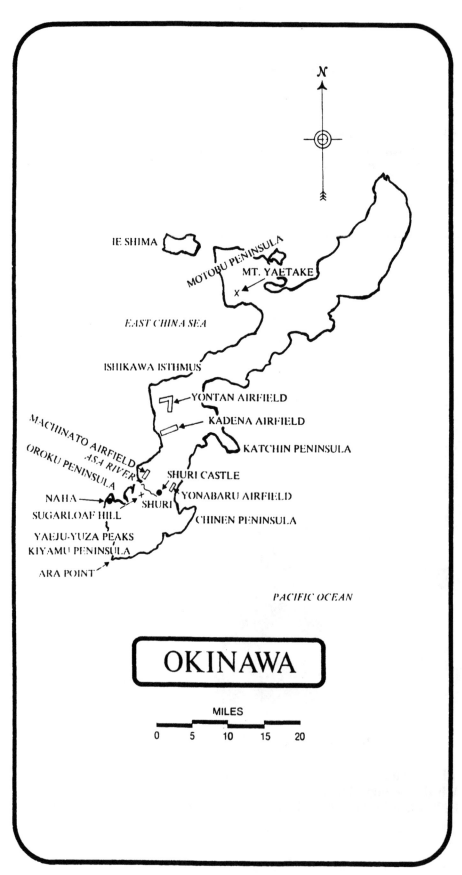

IE SHIMA

MOTOBU PENINSULA

MT. YAETAKE

EAST CHINA SEA

ISHIKAWA ISTHMUS

YONTAN AIRFIELD

KADENA AIRFIELD

MACHINATO AIRFIELD
ASA RIVER
OROKU PENINSULA

KATCHIN PENINSULA

SHURI CASTLE

NAHA

YONABARU AIRFIELD

SHURI

SUGARLOAF HILL

CHINEN PENINSULA

YAEJU-YUZA PEAKS
KIYAMU PENINSULA

ARA POINT

PACIFIC OCEAN

OKINAWA

MILES

0   5   10   15   20

National Archives

REFUSES TO GO DOWN. 12 April 1945

The massive damage to the USS Lindsey (DM-32) when two Japanese suicide planes found their mark on her in action near Mae Shima off Okinawa. Her forward magazine exploded , shearing away some 60 feet off the bow and leaving only twisted and gagged steel with many of her crew killed and wounded. Only the " ALL BACK FULL " ordered by Commander Chambers prevented the presure of inrushing water from collapsing the fireroom bulkhead and sinking the ship. She was towed to Kerama Retto for temporary repairs.

National Archives

USS LINDSEY SURVIVES DESPITE DOUBLE SUICIDE ATTACK - Twice hit by suicide planes in action near Mae Shima off Okinawa on 12 April 1945, her bow and forward hull section twisted beyond recongition, the minelayer USS LINDSEY still stayed afloat despite loss of 50 men killed and 57 wounded. This picture shows the ship plowing her way through the water soon after the attack.

National Archives

USS LINDSEY DM-32 damaged by Jap suicide planes while operating off Kerama Retto.

96

USS AARON WARD (DM-34)

These photos show the massive damaged by suicide attack of 5 Japanese planes while operating off Kerama Retto , 3 May 1945. Through the night, her crew fought to save the ship. At 2106, Shannon (DM-25) arrived and took Aaron Ward in tow and early on the morning of 4 May , she arrived at Kerama Retto for temporary repairs.

National Archives

USS COMFORT (AH-6)
3 April at Okinawa,Ryukyus

(at right)   3 May 1945
at Guam, escorted in by the
USS Fraser (DM-24), the
USS COMFORT (AH-6) awaits
personnel from the ambulances
and busses to remove the dead
and injured as result of Japanese
suicide diver while on station off
Okinawa, 28 April 1945.

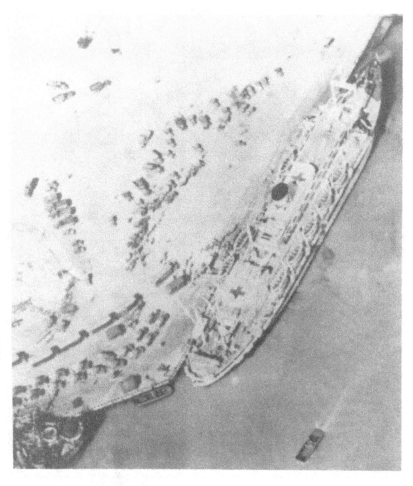

U.S. Navy Photo

THE JAPANESE BAKA (fool) BOMB
weapon of desperation

Many types of planes were used by the Japanese in suicidal attacks at the Pacific Fleet but the Baka bomb shown here was the only plane specially designed for the purpose. Kamikaze (divine wind) or suicide pilots started to operate on a large scale for the first time at Leyte. The wave of Kamikazes reached its frenzied height during the three month battle of Okinawa. The suicide planes took a large toll of shipping and men but were unable to halt our advance towards the home islands and the heavy almost day and night naval and aerial fight for Okinawa ended in victory for the American forces, with many of the Kamikazes being " splashed ".

National Archives

National Archives

JAPANESE BAKA BOMB IN FLIGHT

National Archives

National Archives

**Kerama Retto, Ryukyu Islands 6 January 1945 Anti-aircraft action
USS Logan Victory (ammo. ship) hit behind point**

Courtesy John E. Moser   USS Strength AM-309

Exploding contact mine snagged in sweep gear. November 1945

Destroyers sortie from Buckner Bay, Okinawa as typhoon approached. September 1945

Courtesy John E. Moser   USS Strength AM-309

YMS-478

In September, the USS *Fraser* DM-24 operated with sweep units clearing mines in Kii Suido, in Wakayama anchorage, and off the Pacific coast of the Japanese islands. While anchored in Wakanoura Wan on the 17th. and 18th., *Fraser* weathered a typhoon whose 100-knot gusts forced her to use her engines to ease the strain on her anchor. During the night of 17 September 1945 the typhoon hit full force with winds around 125 MPH. The YMS-478 had two anchors out forward and both engines going full speed ahead into the wind. First one anchor broke, than the other. At this point the YMS-478 drifted across the bay until she hit the coastal rocks. The starboard side caved in and the YMS-478 floundered on the rocks. All this took place sometime around 2:00 am, on the morning of 18 September 1945 which lasted for six to seven hours. When the storm abated, *Fraser* sent out a party to aid survivors and to remove confidential gear and publications from YMS-478 which had broached and capsized. Two crewmen, *Ensign Delbert Lamont Federickson* and *Buford Monroe Stallings, Coxswain*, lost their lives and the survivors were taken aboard the *Fraser* at 1800. Later the YMS-478 was completely destroyed by setting off a demolition charge under her hull.

courtest of Charles W. Nelson YMS-478

National Archives

THE SECRETARY OF THE NAVY
WASHINGTON

OCT 31 1945

Honorable J. H. Bankhead
United States Senate
Washington, D. C.

Dear Senator Bankhead:

Thank you for sending me the letter from the members
of the crew of the USS REVENGE. They are quite right
in their statement that their ship was the first to
enter Tokyo Bay as part of the occupation fleet.

However, we can find no record here of any other ship,
including the USS SAN DIEGO, being named as the first
Allied ship to enter the Bay, nor of any kind of award,
monetary or otherwise, being given to any other vessel
for that reason.

Sincerely yours,

James Forrestal

HONOLULU STAR BULLETIN - 1946

First Ship In Tokyo Bay, USS Revenge AM-110

The first Allied ship to enter Tokyo bay arrived at Pearl Harbor yesterday on the last leg of her voyage to the U.S. She carries a name to fit the history she made that day. *USS Revenge.*

On the morning of Aug. 28, 1945, the *Revenge*, a 220-foot minesweeper, led the victory "V" formation of sweepers which cleared the way into Tokyo bay for the *USS San Diego* and the Third fleet under Admiral Halsey. During the months since the surrender, while other ships have been receiving postwar plaudits in the shelter of American waters, the *Revenge* has been aiding in historys greatest minesweeping campaign. Since the campaign is now nearing completion, the *Revenge* has been able to return, the navy said.

At daylight on Aug. 28, the *Revenge* with Lt. Cdr. James L. Jackson of Atlanta, Ga., in command, steamed her minesweeping gear and entered Tokyo bay, followed in close formation by the minesweepers *Token*, *Tumult* and *Pochard*. Although the Jap pilot aboard had charts of the minefields and nets across the channel, the crew of the *Revenge* was alerted for anything.

Carefully the ships probed what the Japs said were safe channels, according to yesterday's announcement. By 8 in the morning, the entrance channel had been thoroughly checked; no mines were found, so the *Revenge* and her sister ships started to sweep safe areas in which the big ships of the fleet could anchor.

Pulled With Batteries

Tokyo bay was the most important, but not the first "first" for the *Revenge*. Before the main invading fleet arrived at Kwajalein, the *Revenge* was inside the lagoon sweeping away the Jap mine defenses. There and in later invasions the minesweepers dueled with shore batteries and splashed Jap planes which were trying to save the minefields for bigger prey.

The *Revenge* was at Okinawa clearing minefields nine days before the day set for the invasion, the navy said. There, last March 23, her career was almost ended. Sweeping a dangerous shallow field, the formation lead ship, *USS Skylark*, hit a mine. A sheet of flames rolled from under her starboard side to the top of the bridge. The *Skylark* leaned heavily to port and started to sink. Some one had to reach her and rescue the survivors. But approach from either side was dangerous; the explosion of one mine meant that others still lurked unswept near the sinking ship. The *Revenge* and the *Sage* each picked a side and swept into the *Skylark*. In that dash, the *Revenge* found no mines, the *Sage* one. Two patrol craft followed the *Revenge* and picked up survivors as the *Skylark* sank.

Anti-Sub Patrol

Later in the Okinawa campaign, the *Revenge* was shifted to the "ping" line patrol against Jap submarines. In the early morning of April 9, her radar picked up a small "pip" about a thousand yards away. Simultaneously, the sound operator reported underwater propeller noises. Depth charges, 40 and 20 millimeter guns were manned. A searchlight spotted the target, a small floating object that could have been a midget Jap sub or an Army "duck". With the second possibility in mind, the crew held its fire.

Suddenly, the small craft dashed out of the searchlight and headed for the *Revenge*. At 100 yards she was detected and this time definitely identified as a Jap suicide boat. Before guns could be brought into action, the craft had raced within 25 yards of the *Revenge*. Shells poured into the suicide boat as she streaked under the bow. Seconds later the craft blew up in a flash of flame. The crew of the *Revenge* waited for the explosions from dynamite which the Jap boat might have hurled in the dark, but nothing happened.

Six Planes Attack

Returning to minesweeping tasks, the *Revenge*, and five other minecraft were sweeping off Okinawa last April 16, when six Jap planes attacked to break up the precise formation on which the success of minesweeping operation depends. "Cooly the little ships maintained their positions, shot down five of the six , and continued on course, cleaning up the minefield," the announcement said.

From Okinawa, the *Revenge* swept north into the China Sea, then made her historic Tokyo entrance. Since then, the *Revenge* and 300 other American minecraft have been clearing occupation ports of thousands of Japanese and American mines, the navy reported.

August 22, 1945

To all hands ;

On the first anniversary of the THOMAS E. FRASER (DM-24) you may look back on the record of events performed by her with enviable and justifiable pride. It is a record of all missions assigned having been accomplished and done well.

To many of you who came on board a year ago, this was your first ship and in many ways a far different life then you were normally accustomed to. The manner in which each one of you have adapted yourself to this life reflects credit on each one of you for which ideals we engaged in this bitter conflict. That you were able to do so, meant the rapid and coherent weldment into a fighting team to man the ship in which you serve and enables her to take her place in the U.S. Navy anywhere and anytime. You and your ship were ready and have continued to be ready for all assignments.

For my own part, I have been with you only a short period and can only share in your past excellent performance by the records, but I assure you, its a glorious one that gives me great satisfaction and makes me proud to be with you.

The future still holds much for all of us before fulfillment of homeward bound becomes real, but that time will come. Until it does come, each of us, for this is your ship, will continue to leave a record surpassing that of the first year of service, and will make it always a record for those who someday will follow us on board, to be proud of and to live up to.

N.B. Atkins
Commander, U.S. Navy
Commanding

Commander Atkins
addressing some
crewmembers of
the Fraser (DM-24)

courtesy
Milton Hackett

Foo Sees The Light

Icky Foo was born of smoke
And grime at Iwo Jima,
But since has nearly sunk from sight
Like the face of that old Shima.
Icky's eyes grew bright again
To see the concentration
Of lights, and tents, and huts, and ships
Built since the conflagration.

Tears swelled in his beady eyes
Once filled with mischief, greed & hate.
A lump choked off his speech
That had been so taut of late.
He groped for words to soften up
The attitudes he'd molded
Into men of the Fearless Fraser
Who had griped, & groaned, & scolded.

His change of heart, tho' slow to come
Seemed genuine enough,
He'd smooth the edges down a bit
That had been so rough 'n tough.
" How did I get this way," he mused ;
" Being a ' spirit ' myself ? "
" How did I happpen to be such a mean
And a devilish, nautical elf"

But then inside he felt a twinge
As a mortal whose conscience is questioned.
And he said to himself,
" Here's the answer, by heck,
To what I thot was my indigestion! "
" I find I've a 'small voice' within me, like you,
And I'll name my tormentor
It's our friend (?) , Puny Lou! "

Howdy Dow

THE NATION'S YOUTH (PAST TENSE USED HERE) ANSWERS THE CALL!.

"So------ You Boys want to join the Navy!?"

RECRUITING OFFICE

AT LAST - JAPANESE SURRENDER

Just one week ago today, we received the great news that the Japs had at last given up the fight. To most of us it meant the beginning of the end of an epoch in our lives and the return to what we hope will be a normal life. All of us will , I believe , feel regret when the time comes to leave the FRASER- a little bit of everyone will remain with the ship when we go over the side for the last time. Likewise we who have fought and played together will retain a bit of the ship when we scatter to take up our various peacetime pursuits.

Many of us are inclined to call the FRASER a " lucky " ship because we have come through the Iwo Jima and Okinawa campaigns unscathed when so many other ships were sunk or damaged. In analyzing our " luck " a bit however, we might find that it was in a large part due to the courage, skill and " guts " of the individual members of the crew, each doing his job a little better then he has ever done it before, that has pulled us through every action.

In any case, we have come to the final curtain. In a few more days the last act will be over, and we as members of the cast will soon be laying our costumes aside and looking forward to the day when we can resume our normal roles. The fact that the enemy has been so completely defeated, that he has surrendered, gives us the satisfaction of knowing that our part was well played - and before an appreciative audience.

If I could speak representing the ship, I would say " well done to all hands." we have come through a lot together - we have fought and won together. We have accomplished our purpose and will soon be ready to separate and return to where we belong.

" OUR STORY "

" Post the watch, Mr. Hackett ". A shifting of feet as the watch marched off, a salute and then " The watch is set, Sir." It was just a year ago today that we were standing on the fantail under a broiling Boston sun listening to those words which officially placed the USS Thomas E. Fraser in the fighting fleet. Officially that day marked the FRASER's birth but actually is that right? Months before many of us had been sent to Bath to supervise construction ; most of us "sweated it out" in those ovens called Quonset Huts at Norfolk. Still others were at school. Yes, much had gone before but it was not until that afternoon of commissioning that all of us, ship, crew and officers were finally brought together and started on our cruise. Since then, during the past year, we have stayed for the most part the same unit and so, since the story of the FRASER is the story of a team, let's take a look at what we've done and as a starting point we'll take 22 August 1944.

That was quite a day, all right with the excitement and the ceremony, numerous friends and relatives asking questions about gadgets and gismos which as yet some of us had never seen before but we told them anyway that they were "hush-hush", and then that first night of getting settled. It was a lucky day too; for us, for the fleet and for Boston. The last mentioned certainly saw enough of the FRASER - six weeks of us (kindly brought about by the Chief Engineer and his snipes) and we made every minute count in one way or another. Anyday you could find the minemen busy with the tracks. The quartermasters installing ashtrays all around the bridge, the electricians putting up fans and "joe-pots" and the shipfitters busy patching up the stern. And any night- well, it was a bit hard to keep track of all of us then. However, it was a great time and soon we learned our way around the ship and started pulling together. By the end of our stay we were really clicking, everything was aboard and the shadow of shakedown lay before us, the big test. We were sorry to leave Boston and in many ways Boston hated to see us go, but we were ready and willing, anxious to see how we would compare with our sister ships.

" Let go one and three, all back one ", and we were off. Looking back on it now this trip was not too rough but to some it certainly was no millpond. The time was spent in last minute check-ups to see that all was in readiness for those inspections given to all new ships on the shakedown.

At Bermuda, everyday we'd steam out that long channel ("combat, where is the next buoy" ?) for gunnery exercises, sub runs, engineering and damage control drills, and only too frequently that operation which is "old stuff" to us now- G.Q. Sooner or later, practically all the officers answered a hurried summons to the bridge. The engineers managed to make, black, white and gray smoke with amazing regularity but always just at the wrong minute. The foc's'le seemed never to be able to " get out one and two " quite soon enough ; Combat couldn't find the buoys but resorted to a spy system; the gunners, a lighting bunch preferred the plane to the sleeve as a target, and everybody seemed too slow in getting to G.Q. Those were some of the troubles we had but there were laughs too. The day the Chief Pharmacist's mate went puffing up the ladder to the bridge with an aspirin for the Captain; the time the word was passed " all hands once around the upper deck " and Doc followed by Mr. Cogshall were seen tumbling furiously round the minetracks and the liberty , especially the first one in which the SMITH took a drubbing.

Bermuda was a really beautiful spot with its cool green countryside dotted with white roofed cottages, its winding dirt roads and its ever present colonial atmosphere. Having been at sea all of two weeks we considered ourselves " old salts " and when liberty time rolled around there was no doubt about the outcome. The time passed quickly and before we knew it , the two final inspections had come and were passed with flying colors- and then we were off again, presumably for Boston. Fate (or the Bureau) decided otherwise, however, and our spirits slumped as the scuttlebutt got around that we were Norfolk bound.

Disappointed though we were, not to get back to Boston, it was nevertheless a great feeling to be steaming up the Chesapeake, back in the States again. During the previous month just about everyone had had a chance to make mistakes (and did) except the minemen. Now they came into the limelight. But on the whole, our initial efforts at our specialty were excellent even though Mr. Mc Connel and Mr. Bush had a few trying moments. As a matter of fact our record was better than those who'd gone before us and we were all amazed at what we could do. Equally amazing was our first real practice shore bombardment in which the gunnery department truly distinguished itself. We thought they'd gone a little too far, though, when " down five thousand " came over the phones but then everyone is a little off, sometime or another.

So over we went to Norfolk for post-shakedown availability. Our stay there was pretty uneventful, however, except for the fact there was no leave. Some of us nevertheless left (with sad results). Thanksgiving produced a bright spot, though, with the first of Mr. Gleason's and Chief Holmes' feasts.

Soon after came the day- the day that started us of on our travels. In a way we were glad and proud to be shoving off but as we steamed out through the gray mist past the familiar Chamberlain Hotel , we all felt that lump in our throats. Outwardly the only way the FRASER could say "good bye " was the three blasts on the whistle and three black puffs of smoke but inwardly we were all thinking very much of those we were leaving behind.

The FRASER's first stop was Guantanamo, Cuba, a big, hot base which then looked pretty desolate to us but now it would seem like heaven. There we picked up our first job, escort of the USS ALASKA, a new battle-cruiser. With her following behind (as only fitting !), we steamed southwest to the Panama Canal. We arrived in the afternoon and tied up to the USS Bauer, the first of our sister ships that we'd met. That night we had liberty- oh , what a liberty. It started out for most of us as a sightseeing tour of Cristobal, a rather intriguing looking town. The sights proved to be well worth seeing, especially one certain street which for well known reasons was jammed to capacity. As it turned out, the coxswains and electricians mates did very well there. Next day saw the Thomas E. Fraser underway again, this time under the expert guidance of a pilot who, beside giving orders to the helm, engines, and donkeys on the locks, managed to keep up a running description of points of interest over the PA system. That was the first time the bridge was treated to a glimpse of a certain GM striker's lovely legs as we took advantage of the fresh water to scrub down.

Safely through the Canal, the three of us, ALASKA, BAUER and FRASER churned quietly up the Pacific to San Diego. Nothing much happened except for a storm but by then we were used to that treatment. " Dago " proved to be another shakedown without much liberty and soon we were off, really bound for war. Our charges this time were transports loaded with WACS, who upon closer examination turned out to be hairy Seabees, but not until after all the binoculars on board got quite a workout. (Those signalmen sure have some eyes!). Midway during the trip was December 25th- for some of us the first Christmas afloat. In true Navy fashion we had a Christmas tree flying from the yard arm and a tremendous feast complete with Santa Claus (Gibbons-style) and all the trimmings. Most, if not all, of our Christmas presents had arrived and the day was spent eagerly opening them and listening to carols on the radio.

Several days later saw the " Fighting Fraser " nose up to a mooring buoy in Pearl Harbor, her last real stop before her initial action at Iwo Jima. Hawaii, as we so well remember, had lots to offer; a warm balmy climate just right for movies topside, wonderful swimming at Waikiki, magnificent views such as the Pali and Diamond Head, and numerous entertainments furnished by the YMCA. Then too, there were the delights of Kahoolawe , that much pounded island, but despite a large share of hard work, the FRASER made many a good liberty. One guard mail P.C. and several coxswains can testify to that. But the fun couldn't last forever and before we knew it , January was almost gone and the FRASER was on her way once more.

Enroute to Eniwetok, we made one short stop for mail at Johnston Island which was a prelude to the general appearance of all Pacific Isles. Nothing more then a dot in the ocean. Johnston was all sand and Army huts, baked by the sun and yet teaming with activity. Eniwetok turned out similar (the trip was not too exciting) except that there the harbor was a hundred times bigger than the atoll. By that time word had gotten around that we were Iwo-bound and the FRASER " turned to " on stores, ammunition and fuel with new vigor. From Eniwetok to Saipan and then north we went , and on 19 February 1945, the THOMAS E. FRASER found herself off Iwo Jima, about to commence her career of action.

During the preceding night, starshells from the pre-invasion bombardment had been visible to us as our convoy approached the Island. At about 0300, General Quarters was sounded and as we hurried up to our battle stations, each of us wondered just what action would be like and said a prayer or two. Dawn found us on a screening station with a ringside seat to the greatest bombardment yet in the Pacific. What had been a calm green little island, was now tawny-brown , pock-marked, and over hung with a vast cloud of gray smoke. Battleships, cruisers, destroyers and aircraft poured shells, rockets, and fire into that strip of earth repeatedly and constantly. Suddenly the barrage let up and little assault boats, each leaving a straight white wake, streaked into the beach. Then the shooting commenced again. This time a little higher up the ridge so as not to hit our troops. So it went all morning without respite and little by little the line of fire rose from the beach up to the ridge and over the airfield, the Marines first objective. All was going well and to us it seemed more of a big show then the grim reality of war. Next day, or D plus 1, the FRASER was ordered in to bombard. Our assignment was Mount Suribachi, the tunneled stronghold of the Japs on the southern tip of the island. Taking station close to the beach, we cruised back and forth lobbing shells into caves , pillboxes, and the like. Of course we were constantly on guard for counter-fire but none occurred and all went off well for us, but not for the Japs! Night fell and with it started that continuous starshell illumination which became so familiar to us. One night that we were firing, news come that a party of Japs was attempting to swim around the Marines lines and attack from the rear. The FRASER was ready, however, and covered the area with "stars " which sealed the fate of those Nips. So it went for the better part of three weeks ; screening, bombarding, fueling, and always, it seemed, handling ammunition. (see article of statistics). A few of the more outstanding highlights were : rescuing two Marines in a " duck "; firing several ill-aimed shots across the bow of a battlewagon ; repelling our first air attack with the cry " give her six, Dick ". Perhaps the height of the FRASER's career at Iwo occurred that day we anchored just offshore and proceeded to bombard to port and paint the starboard side all at the same time. At last one day, our job was done, and the order came to leave. The trip down to Ulithi was indeed pleasant; no G.Q.'s, no helmets and a general feeling of having " proved ourselves ". The THOMAS E. FRASER had graduated from a rookie to a veteran!

Ulithi- need any more be said ? Just another atoll, mostly water, and a great many ships. We did, however, get a good rest and with movies topside and a single liberty (the "two can of beer" kind). The general monotony was broken. While there we acquired a dog and almost lost one of the officers who seemed to prefer the beach to the ship.

By that time March had rolled around and Easter was a few weeks away. Once again the Fighting Fraser headed north for an operation which supposedly would be " bigger but easier " than Iwo. The name of the invasion site was Okinawa.

Our first glimpse of Kerama Retto, that group of islands just west of Okinawa, came early one morning late in March as our little group steamed in to clear the way for the " big boys ". That old feeling of tenseness cropped up once more as we inched between the islands, expecting any minute to be on the receiving end of a shell or bomb. But nothing happened and our work progressed smoothly, even to a point of doing some shore bombardment ourselves. That pre-invasion week crept by slowly due to those nocturnal " bogies " which kept us up.

Finally " Love Day " arrived and hopes rose as the favorable reports of the invasion came in. By this time, needless to say, the Fraser's nerves were on edge. The result of bagging three planes and being narrowly missed by the fourth. Consequently the day we set off for Guam was indeed a happy one. Our stay at that sunny isle was all too pleasant with its frequent liberty parties, movies, and fresh provisions. But it couldn't last forever and before we know it , the Fraser was back at the front. We returned to Okinawa just in time to be in on one of the biggest air raids there. After playing hide and seek with a " Betty " all evening, we were abruptly ordered away and found that the USS COMFORT , a hospital ship , had been hit and that it was our job to care for her. So - back to Guam again. Our stay that time was even shorter then before. And when we got back to " Okie ", it turned out to be for good and for the real thing. For the whole month of May, the Thomas E. Fraser took her place among that gallant band of ships on the " picket line ". The routine became little more than eat, sleep, stand a watch, and go to battle stations. Several times we stood at G.Q. all night and the average sleep allowance dropped to four hours per day. During that period we bagged an additional four planes, saw and heard many more (including those two " TBF's " one night, who suddenly became " Kates ") ; and yet came through unscathed. Little by little, the situation improved as our troops drove back the Japanese and at last it was over- perhaps the Navy's most heroic stand of the war.

Since that time, the Fraser has been far from idle but unfortunately it's not " the news that's fit to print ". One item, however, is that Captain Woodman who put the ship in commission has been relieved by Captain Atkins. Captain Woodman returns to the States while Captain Atkins is carrying on the good work here on the fighting front.

This, then, is the story of the Fraser during her first year. She's a good ship and a fighting ship but it's not the rivets, nor the steel that make her so. No, it's the crew, all of us, each doing his own specific job to the best of his ability and each job fitting into the teamwork of the whole. And that is the way it has been. It is not the engineers, or the gunners mate; officers, or seamen; cook or yeomen, who alone make the ship. Its the teamwork of one and all, from the top right on down.

****

The views expressed herein are considered to be accurate and factual, but are not to be construed in any manner as representing the official news of the Navy Department, U.S. Navy or any other government agency. Reprinting in hometown newspaper is permissable.

NOTES AFTER ONE YEAR IN COMMISSION

When we came " to war" I promised you several things---one and the main one was, " to take you into action, and with your support to take you out, and to bring you all without exception after this war, home to your wives, your mothers, or to your sweethearts." You have done your part well, and there has been no Captain prouder of his command than I.

It is therefore difficult to write this knowing that very shortly I will be detached. Even after five years at sea in this war, I leave with a heavy heart because I have grown to love my ship. My greatest recompense is that my relief, Comdr. ATKINS, will fulfill the other half of my promise " to bring you all back."

One year ago we were ordered by the Secretary of the Navy to ready ourselves and our ship to seek out and destroy by day or night our able and ruthless enemy. We have worked to that end, and though at times it appeared as though " the old man with scythe " was just around the corner, we have not only come through, but come through with colors flying.

We have seen many of our ships and comrades lost during our action with the enemy, and we have learned the hard way that the price of survival is eternal vigilance. Some of you have been rewarded by decorations for that vigilance. I regret deeply that all could not be decorated. My most earnest admonition is still the same-in battle you react as you have been trained- if you must make mistakes, make them in training, for you can recoup in business, an army may retreat to fight another day, but at sea there is no second chance. No longer may colors be honorably struck against great odds. Today you must fight to win, and fight until your very ship disappears beneath the waters. We must never give up the ship.

I believe sincerely that we have advanced a long way toward fulfilling that remark of Captain HARTWIG, USN (a classmate of Comdr. THOMAS E. FRASER) who said prior to our commissioning , " if the ship is half as good as Tommy was a man- it will be the fightingest ship in this or any man's Navy."

R.J. WOODAMAN

NO SMALL PEANUTS

NOTE :

There is one species of creature that infests this world which always bobs up at the end of anything with a fist full of statistics weather it be wars, football games, clearance sales, or anniversaries of DM's. It seems to be a specially constituted type of being, different from the rest of the human race, one which thrives on figures. We suspect that it has an adding machine for a heart, a thin numeral soup for a blood stream and for its Bible a table of logarithims. It loves to lay things end-to-end. The following article represents the efforts of one such mental slide rule, who until now has kept his true nature secret, but who couldn't resist the temptation to add up figures for the FRASER's anniversary.

ED.

The FRASER sure is a " going " concern. She keeps going farther and farther away from home. At this writing she has travelled over 55,000 miles. She's as far away from Boston as she's ever been, but that's only about 6,500 miles as a lazy crow would fly, that is , by the great circle route which passes within 800 miles of the North Pole. She's what the papers refer to as a " light Unit " which might give some people the mistaken notion that she's " small peanuts ". She isn't though and there are some interesting figures to prove it.

The snipes, for example, have burned up about 150 tank cars of fuel oil, well over 3 million gallons, most of it without making smoke, too. They've made three and one quarter million gallons of fresh water or about enough to fill twenty-one normal sized swimming pools. Of that amount 2,300,000 gallons have been used for showers, galley, drinking and so forth. We could have used twice as much, but it is still a lot. Each of the two propellors has revolved something like 32,000,000 times. The amount of work done by those props is tremendous, 67,500,000 horse power-hours. That's enough to lift the FRASER and everybody on her, 370 miles straight up ; and it would be a good thing too, cooler and no Kamikaze.

About twelve thousand rounds of ammunition have been lugged aboard, and some of it off. Most of it , though, has gone out the business end of the guns to the discomfort of the Sons of Heaven. Over twenty-eight hundred rounds were fired in training and practices, and pretty close to 6,500 were fired at the enemy, ashore and aloft. That doesn't include what the machine guns have used.

The result is that the scoreboard on the bridge shows seven planes downed, two shore bombardments, and around fifteen mines exploded or sunk.

We've been at General Quarters 123 times because of air raids, and the longest one kept us there for ten miserable hours. The longest General Quarters, though, was at Iwo Jima that first day, of her initial action. That one lasted eighteen hours.

Despite the gripes about Navy coffee, about twelve hundred cups are consumed every day. Some people will drink anything.

The ship's store has sold over two million cigarettes, eleven and a half tons of candy, 10,000 bars of soap, and enough stationary for 80,000 letters. The chewing gum sold has caused FRASER JAWS to clamp down some 250,000,000 times in the last year.

These studies have disclosed an alarming condition in one group of men on this ship- the ping-jockeys. During the past twelve months they've listened to 2,685,000 pings, or 335,000 per man. The best authorities agree that a human being can listen to no more than 250,000 per year without losing his mind. We are led to the conclusion, which confirms suspicion we've had all along ; that the soundmen are all " ping-happy ". The radarmen, of course, were a hopeless case from the very start, so the less said about their statistics the better.

The radiomen, so far, have listened to 105 million dots and 89.5 million dashes on the scheds alone. Clearly they, too, are near the breaking point.

The ship's barbers have each given nearly three thousand haircuts, the laundry has washed 65,000 shirts and an equal number of pants, the deck force has washed down thirty five miles of deck, and if the ship were rigged for sailing, the wind expanded by the bos'n mates would be enough to take us clear back to Boston in record time.

" THE CRACKER BARREL "

In Kerama Retto one fine sunny morning Doctor Porter the ship's " Jack of all Trades ", had his first important case. Rosemary, then the FRASER's mascot, was deathly ill and needed immediate attention. So with unsurpassable skill our young Doctor Killdare performed the operation... an enema !! The little beast showed remarkable changes, yet everytime she opened her mouth the air was filled with large bubbles. To make a long story short, her condition grew worse, and one dark stormy night she was " Deep sixed ". Actually it was no one's fault....just too much soap.

The bridge is always complaining about keeping the red light off in Mount Two. The problem is now solved, " Red " Yates wears dark glasses after sunset.

Koontz, the ship's baker and also the crew's outstanding example of heat rash, has been continually congratulated on his tasty raisin bread. Upon closer examination it was found that his raisins had legs and could walk !!

The biggest surprise in months came when Seaman, oversized lip flapper, made Chief. By pure coincidence, Mr. White at the same time received a new fan over his sack.

During a stores working party not long ago, as the workers were diligently bringing the food aboard, some wise guy hit the Chief Commissary Steward in the head with one of those cadavres they happen to call meat. It was the first time in months that the old boy has come face to face with his own food. No one will ever forget the day he tried to pass off that fossilized chicken on the crew. The birds themselves looked as though they flew all the way from the States on a non-stop flight. A crisis finally occurred, everybody complained so badly that it aroused the attention of the higher ups. Eventually Doctor Poter looked at the birds, Mr. Gleason looked, the Chief looked, the messcooks looked, even the birds looked and were ashamed at what they saw. Frankly and with all kidding aside, it was the biggest concentration of bones since the day Mr. Hackett was caught sunning on the boat deck.

Inspite of what some may think, carrying ammunition aboard is not only monotonous but dangerous as well. Shackleford can vouch for that. Months ago, when the bogies were plentiful and amno scarce because of constant firing, as usual ALL Hands (excluding Chiefs, First Class, some seconds, essential ship workers plus the remaining Gold Bricks) were taking on projectiles. Shackleford, doing his share of the work, was carrying one also when he slipped on the wet deck endangering the lives of his shipmates. Mr. "Trackit" realizing the seriousness of the situation acted on impulse ; he threw Shackleford over the side and fined the projectile for being so careless.

You may be interested to learn the latest about our chum, that calculating " C " Division Commando, Mr. Cogshall. Several weeks back some unknown admirer, showing pity, sent our " Leader " a fashionable wig of Louis the 14th. The hell of it was, Louis got sore and took it back on the 15th....Indian Giver !!!

Although it did no good, Harry Hagle, eigth wonder of the world, shaved off his beard, but he still can't make Chief. The only logical step now is to regrow it again.

Gibbons, fat and aging circus clown, who is noted for his size beard, bald spot and juicy tabacco plugs, has the strange and sloppy habit of exposing his skivvie shorts although fully clothed. Obviously he misinterpretes the order "Air Bedding ." Proportionally maybe, the two articles are similiar in dimention, one thing is certain, both have the same color.... a mouse grey tint.

" THE CRACKER BARREL " (Cont'd)

Condon, Fire Controlman First Class and also New Jersey's boy wonder still defends his native village against all exaggerated ridicule by foreigners. For those who might be interested, Kenilworth is the only town in the country where the lamp lighter has the additional duty of cleaning the Owl droppings off the town clock so that people can read time.

There are some innocent and naive characters aboard who to this day believe that the wrapped parcel of the K ration's Supper Unit labeled "Scotch Tissue", is writing paper! Jones boys take note

****

ANNIVERSARY MENU

Cream of Tomato Soup
Young Roast Turkey
Whipped Potatoes
Yellow Whole Corn
Young Green Peas
Cranberry Sauce
Raisin Dressing
Dill Pickles
Ice Cream
&
Birthday Cake
Iced Tea
Cigarettes

ALLEN M. SUMNER CLASS DESTROYER

NAME	HULL #	BUILDER	LAID DOWN	LAUNCHED	COMM.	DM	STRICKEN	REMARKS
Robert H. Smith	735	BIW	1/10/44	5/25/44	8/4/44	BIW 6/44	2/26/71	* DM-23
Thomas E. Fraser	736	BIW	1/31/44	6/10/44	8/22/44	BIW 6/44	11/1/70	* DM-24
Shannon	737	BIW	2/14/44	6/24/44	9/8/44	BIW 6/44	11/1/70	* DM-25
Harry F. Bauer	738	BIW	3/6/44	7/3/44	9/22/44	BIW 6/44	8/15/71	* DM-26
Adams	739	BIW	3/20/44	7/23/44	10/10/44	BIW 6/44	12/1/70	* DM-27
Tolman	740	BIW	4/10/44	8/13/44	10/27/44	BIW 6/44	12/1/70	* DM-28
Henry A. Wiley	749	BSI	11/28/43	4/21/44	8/31/44	BSI 6/44	10/15/70	* DM-29
Shea	750	BSI	12/28/43	5/20/44	9/30/44	BSI 6/44	9/1/73	* DM-30
J.William Ditter	751	BSI	1/25/44	6/4/44	10/28/44	BSI 6/44	10/11/45	* DM-31
Lindsey	771	BSP	9/12/43	3/5/44	8/20/44	BSP 6/44	10/1/70	* DM-32
Gwin	772	BSP	10/31/43	4/9/44	8/20/44	BSP 6/44	10/22/71	** DM-33
Aaron Ward	773	BSP	12/12/43	5/5/44	10/28/44	BSP 6/44	10/11/44	* DM-34

Mine Division Seven : USS Robert H. Smith (DM-23)
USS Thomas E. Fraser (DM-24)
USS Shannon (DM-25)
USS Harry F. Bauer (DM-26)

Mine Division Eight : USS Adams (DM-27)
USS Tolman (DM-28)
USS Henry A. Wiley (DM-29)
USS Shea (DM-30)

Mine Division Nine : USS J. William Ditter (DM-31)
USS Lindsey (DM-32)
USS Gwin (DM-33)
USS Aaron Ward (DM-34)

Private Shipyard Symbols

BIW --- Bath Iron Works
BSI --- Bethlehem Steel, Staten Island
BSP --- Bethlehem Steel, San Pedro

*---Sold for Scrap
**--to Turkey--10/22/71
as Mauvenet D-357
Ditter DM-31 sold for scrap 7/1/70
Ward DM-34 sold for scrap 7/1/46
("MAUVENET" met her end when
USS Saratoga accidentally placed two
missles into her bridge.)

ACKNOWLEDGEMENTS

Saga of the USS Thomas E. Fraser.........courtesy of John C. Roach SOM 1c

Happy Birthday Fraser...........................*courtsey of Otis Lecornu Jr. FC3*

USS Revenge AM-110 Letter...............courtsey of Carl W. Allen RDM 1c

Honolulu Star Bulletin-1946 ....courtsey of Carl W. Allen RDM 1c

Cover Photographs.................................courtsey of Bath Iron Works, Bath, Maine

Saga of the USS Walke DD-416.............Naval Historical Center, Navy Yard, Wash. D.C.

Summary of War Damage (Walke).........Charles R. Haberlein,Jr., Naval Historical Center

Lt. Comdr. William Gwin.......................Naval Historical Center, Navy Yard, Wash. D.C.

Exploding contact mine
Destroyer in Pacific typhoon-1945.........courtsey of John E. Moser Comdr. USNR(Retired)

Grounding of USS YMS-478 1945........courtsey of Charles W. Nelson

Midshipmen photographs.......................U.S. Naval Academy, Nimitz Library " Lucky Bag "

Congressman J.William Ditter................Library of Congress Reference and Photo Section

Commander Nevett Brooke Atkins......... Courtest of Milton Hackett collection

Summary of War Damage, "Walke".........Charles R. Haberlein Jr., Naval Historical Center

INDEX

Printed in the USA
CPSIA information can be obtained
at www.ICGtesting.com
JSHW052000150824
68134JS00058B/2657

9 781563 113345